ouR
268.43
LOF
2002

LIVING Our FAITH
Sacraments
Signs of Our Faith

Lourdes Library
Gwynedd Mercy College
P. O. Box 901
Gwynedd Valley, PA 19437-0901

DISCARD

W9-ABR-883

Principal **Consultants**

Dennis J. Bozanich, MBA

Michael Carotta, EdD

Rev. Leonard Wenke, MDiv

Principal **Reviewers**

Mary Lee Becker, MPM

Robert J. Kealey, EdD

M. Annette Mandley-Turner, MS

LOURDES LIBRARY
CURRICULUM COLLECTION
DISCARD

Harcourt
Religion Publishers

Nihil Obstat
Rev. Richard L. Schaefer
Censor Deputatus

Imprimatur
✠ Most Rev. Jerome Hanus, OSB
Archbishop of Dubuque
January 31, 2001
Feast of Saint John Bosco, Patron of Youth and Catholic Publishers

The nihil obstat and imprimatur are official declarations that a book or pamphlet is free of doctrinal or moral error. No implication is contained herein that those who granted the nihil obstat and imprimatur agree with the contents, opinions, or statements expressed.

Our Mission
The primary mission of Harcourt Religion Publishers is to provide the Catholic and Christian educational markets with the highest quality catechetical print and media resources. The content of these resources reflects the best insights of current theology, methodology, and pedagogical research. These resources are practical and easy to use, designed to meet expressed market needs, and written to reflect the teachings of the Catholic Church.

Copyright © 2002 by Harcourt Religion Publishers, a division of Harcourt, Inc.

All rights reserved. No part of this publication may be reproduced or transmitted in any form or by any means, electronic or mechanical, including photocopy, recording, or any information storage and retrieval system, without permission in writing from the publisher.

Requests for permission to make copies of any part of this work should be mailed to Permissions Department, Harcourt, Inc., 6277 Sea Harbor Drive, Orlando, Florida 32887-6777.

New Revised Standard Version Bible: Catholic Edition copyright © 1993 and 1989 by the Division of Christian Education of the National Council of the Churches of Christ in the U.S.A. Used by permission. All rights reserved.

The Name It, Tame It, Claim It process from the *Catholic and Capable* series is used with permission from Resources for Christian Living.

Photography Credits
AP Wide World Photos: Paul Sakuma: 98; **Art Resource:** Erich Lessing: 66; Museo Pio Christiano, Vatican Museums, Vatican State: 87; **Timothy Boone:** 5; **The Crosiers:** Gene Plaisted: 6, 7, 12, 16, 44, 61, 88; **Digital Imaging Group:** Erik Snowbeck: 16, 36, 45, 65, 78; **Jack Holtel:** 4, 10, 17, 25, 26, 28, 29, 40, 54, 88, 99; **Image Bank:** Ken Huang: 78; Vicky Kasala: 34; Tom Stewart: 70; Paul J. Sutton: 62; Mari Taglienti: 96; **Wolfgang Kaehler:** 89; **Liaison International:** James D. Wilson: 21; **The Merton Legacy Trust:** Sibylle Akers: 38; **National Catholic Youth Conference,** St. Louis, Missouri 1999/National Federation for Catholic Youth Ministry, Inc., Washington, DC: 19; **Nicholas Studios:** Nick Falzerano: 64, 95; **PictureQuest:** PhotoEdit/Michael Newman: 42; Stock Boston/Spencer Grant: 76; Stock Boston/Lawrence Migdale: 67; Woodfin Camp & Associates/Anthony Howarth: 57; **PhotoEdit:** Robert Brenner: 46; Myrleen Ferguson Cate: 8, 61, 84; Tom Freeman: 58; Tony Freeman: 34, 39, 46, 48, 98; Spencer Grant: 75; Micheal Newman: 25, 35, 47, 96; Jonathan Nourok: 17, 74; Alan Oddie: 24, James Shaffer: 69; David Young-Wolfe: 34, 78, 82, 96, 101; **Photo Researchers:** Jeff Greenberg: 38; Renee Lynn: 6; Lawrence Migdale: 22; **Stock Boston:** Dorothy Littell Greco: 85; **The Stock Market:** Ronnie Kaufman: 50, 72; Dilip Mehta: 8; Gabe Palmer: 102; David Woods: 72; **Stone:** Z & B Baran: 74; Myrleen Ferguson Cate: 49; Stewart Cohen: 77; Walter Hodges: 15; Kevin Horan: 80; Philip & Karen Smith: 32; James Strachan: 94; Zigy Kaluzny: 90; **Superstock:** 36, 56: **Jim Whitmer Photography:** Jim Whitmer: 14, 48; **W. P. Wittman Photography:** Bill Wittman: 5, 47, 68, 86

Cover Photos
AGI Photographic Imaging; Cleo Photography; Jack Holtel

Feature Icons
Catholics Believe: Jack Holtel; **Opening the Word:** PictureQuest; **Our Christian Journey:** PictureQuest: Chuck Fishman/Contact Press Images

Location and Props
Dayton Church Supply; St. Christopher Catholic School, Vandalia, OH; St. Peter Catholic School, Huber Heights, OH

Printed in the United States of America

ISBN 0-15-900506-X

10 9 8 7 6 5 4

CHAPTER 1

Symbols and Signs

Lord, show us your love and help us recognize you in the signs you give us. Teach us your ways, support us when we feel lost and lonely, and help us work to be better people. Amen.

What Do You Think?

List the kinds of things that make you who you are. Include anything you might use to identify yourself to another person, such as your gender, color of skin, height, body frame, skills, desires, or groups to which you belong.

_____

_____

_____

If someone were to describe you as a person of faith, what words or symbols would he or she use?

_____

_____

_____

Who We Are

We are members of many groups. Some groups are beyond our choice, such as our family and our cultural or ethnic group. The way we style our hair, the music we listen to, the friends we choose, and the schools we attend are ways we identify ourselves. But what about our faith?

Though we are members of many groups and communities, it is our membership in the Body of Christ that should have the greatest impact on our lives.

So how do we identify ourselves as Catholic? As members of the Catholic Church, what objects and actions do we use?

Signs and **Symbols** of Faith

What is your favorite sports team? What is your favorite brand of clothes? Chances are that both are identified by a sign or a symbol. We use signs and symbols every day to express ourselves and to understand others. A **sign** is an object or event that represents or explains something else. It is used to communicate information. A friendly wave is a sign for hello. A big golden arch is the sign of a certain fast-food restaurant. A **symbol** is like a sign, but it has special emotional or spiritual significance. There is something more powerful, more effective, more objectively meaningful about a symbol.

Signs and symbols are especially important in our faith lives. Religious signs and symbols can help us deepen our understanding of God and remind us of what it means to live as followers of Jesus. One of the most important signs of God's presence is the world around us—God's creation. Through creation we experience God's glory and his power.

Opening the Word

For what can be known about God is plain to them, because God has shown it to them.
Ever since the creation of the world his eternal power and divine nature, invisible though they are, have been understood and seen through the things he has made. Romans 1:19–20

Read *Romans 1:19–32* as well as *Exodus 33:18–23, 1 Kings 19:11–13,* and *Luke 24:13–35.* What do these passages tell us about how we experience God?

_____

_____

_____

Our Christian Journey

A New Approach to the Sacraments Augustine was a bishop who lived in the North African town of Hippo. He is best known for explaining Church beliefs, especially in his most famous works, *Confessions* and *The City of God.* Through his writings, Augustine helped deepen our understanding of the sacraments, which he described as sacred signs. He emphasized that God freely and lovingly acts in our lives, and that the sacraments help us recognize and celebrate his presence. Augustine discussed Baptism and Eucharist in particular. In the Sacrament of Baptism, he wrote, we are not changed overnight. Instead, our Baptism begins a lifelong opportunity to become more generous and loving people. Augustine viewed the celebration of the Eucharist in a similar way. He explained that the Sacrament of the Eucharist helps us become new people in Christ. Saint Augustine's feast day is August 28.

For further information:
Read a biography of Augustine, or research his writings in an encyclopedia.

300	450

320
BEGINNING OF INDIA'S GOLDEN AGE

354-430
SAINT AUGUSTINE'S LIFE

379-395
REIGN OF THEODOSIUS THE GREAT, THE LAST EMPEROR OF A UNITED ROMAN EMPIRE

410
GERMANIC TROOPS CONQUER ROME

Catholics have certain symbols or sacred signs called **sacramentals** that make us aware of God's presence in our lives. One of the symbols we use is the crucifix. It speaks to our hearts about Jesus' saving actions and his love for us. Blessings, holy water, candles, the rosary, statues, palm leaves, and ashes are other examples of sacramentals. Sacramentals are usually used with prayer and sometimes with an action, such as the Sign of the Cross or the sprinkling of holy water. Does your family use sacramentals? If you keep a statue of a saint in a special place, or if you pray a blessing before or after meals, you use sacramentals. Perhaps you received a rosary for your First Communion or for your birthday. If so, then you have a sacramental.

Signs and symbols are also a part of our group celebrations within the Church. We often use signs and symbols to help us celebrate Catholic rites. A **rite** is an established procedure for celebrating specific ceremonies in the Church. Among the most important of our Catholic rites are the seven **sacraments**—Baptism, Eucharist, Confirmation, Reconciliation, Anointing of the Sick, Matrimony, and Holy Orders. Through our celebration of the sacraments, Jesus joins with the assembled community in liturgical actions that are signs and sources of God's **grace,** or God's life and loving relationship with us.

The Mission of **Jesus Christ**

The seven sacraments, which have their origin in Christ's words and actions, are his gifts to his Church. In the Gospels we read stories about how Jesus healed people who were sick (see *Luke 4:38–40*), how he forgave people (see *Matthew 9:2–8*), and how he broke bread with his disciples (see *Mark 14:22–25*). Each of these stories reminds us of how Jesus cares for us and how he wants us to live. In our celebration of the sacraments, we participate in the saving actions of Jesus.

After Jesus returned to his Father, the Holy Spirit was sent to help the followers of Jesus continue his work and to strengthen their faith. The first Christians spread the good news of Jesus and God's kingdom. They prayed and worshiped together as Jesus taught them, and they celebrated their faith with the sacred signs and symbols that we call sacraments. The early Church kept Jesus' message and work alive. Through the centuries Christians have continued to share the good news and celebrate the sacraments.

The Church as **Sacrament**

The writer of the Letter to the Ephesians in the New Testament explains how Christians are united in the Lord by describing Christ as the head of the Church and the Church as his Body. (See *Ephesians 1:22–23*.) This image helps us understand how the Church is united with Christ. As members of his Body, we are called to help one another grow closer to God our Father. The Body of Christ needs to be nourished and cared for. In the sacraments Christ meets us in community and touches our lives so that we are strengthened to live as he did.

Catholics Believe

In the sacraments, Christ works in our lives. See Catechism, #1127.

How can Christ change your life through the sacraments?

_____

_____

_____

Share your responses and thoughts with your Faith Partner.

A World Family

Did you know that there are more than a billion members of the Catholic Church worldwide? Wherever they live, Catholics pray together and celebrate the sacraments in their own languages, including Urdu (India), Sinhalese (Sri Lanka), Kikuyu (Kenya), Yoruba (Nigeria), Arabic (Lebanon), and Vietnamese (Vietnam).

Through the sacraments the Holy Spirit makes us a holy people. We form a community of love to strengthen and support one another and do our part to transform the world. We can look forward to a life with God forever in the fullness of his kingdom.

As we participate in our faith community, we may hear people say that the sacraments are "by the Church" and "for the Church." In saying that the sacraments are "by the Church," we mean that the Church itself, the Body of Christ, is a sacrament through which Jesus and the Holy Spirit work to bring to the world God's gifts of grace, forgiveness, and eternal life. At the same time, these seven signs, and particularly the Eucharist, are said to be "for the Church." This means that the sacraments are special opportunities to draw closer to the mystery of our unique relationship with the loving God— one in three Persons, who created us, saved us, and continues to inspire and help us.

We Celebrate

When we celebrate the sacraments, God is blessed and adored. God the Father sends the Spirit to bring us into communion with Christ. Our lives can be changed if we are open to the power of God's grace.

How do you think God's grace can change your life? Think about the kind of person you are. What gifts and talents do you have? What aspects of your life do you struggle with and wish you could improve? Experiencing God's life and love will help you appreciate how special you are in God's eyes. Through the sacraments, especially the Eucharist and Reconciliation, you will experience God's everlasting love. This experience will help change how you view your life and how you view others. If you are tempted to do things that are harmful to yourself or others, such as drinking or smoking, God's grace in the sacraments can give you the strength you need to avoid these actions. If you aren't getting along with family members, the sacraments can help you reconcile with them. Encountering God in the sacraments changes how you see things and ultimately changes how you want to live as a person in the right relationship with God.

A Life
in Christ

We celebrate the sacraments together as the Body of Christ, offering our prayers of thanks and praise. But we don't celebrate these rituals to gain God's favor. We celebrate them to become one with him and with one another. The sacraments are God's gifts to us. Christ has given them in love to his Church.

When we celebrate the sacraments, the Holy Spirit acts through signs and symbols to change our hearts and make it possible for us to become more loving and more generous. These signs and symbols are not merely reminders of God's love; through them the Holy Spirit helps us live our lives as Christians—strengthening us, forgiving our sins, healing us, and enabling us to grow as members of the Body of Christ.

With your Faith Partner, discuss or make a poster showing how you can be a sacrament to others.

WRAP UP

- •As Catholics we have certain signs and symbols that identify who we are and that bring us closer together with God and one another.
- •The sacraments are Christ's gifts to his Church.
- •The sacraments mark us as members of the Catholic Church.
- •When we celebrate the sacraments, the Holy Spirit transforms our lives through God's love.

What questions do you have about this chapter?

_____

_____

_____

Around the Group

Discuss the following question as a group.

What is the difference between an inspiring sunset or a favorite song and the sacraments in bringing a Catholic closer to God and the Christian community?

After everyone has had a chance to share his or her responses, come up with a group answer for the question upon which everyone can agree.

_____

_____

_____

_____

What personal observations do you have about the group discussion and answer? In what ways do you agree?

_____

_____

_____

_____

Briefly...

At the beginning of this chapter, you were asked to describe some of the ways you identify yourself. Based on what you have learned, what signs and symbols do you use to express your faith?

_____

_____

_____

Using Religious Imagination

Expressions of Faith-

Signs and symbols express who we are as individuals and groups. Religious imagination means using language, symbols, and gestures to offer ourselves to God and to recognize how God reveals himself and comes to dwell with us. Religious imagination is a skill that Catholics use often. We use it when we see God in our relationships, recognize signs of God in creation, read the Bible, celebrate the sacraments, and pray with sacramentals in our homes and at church.

Scripture

"I am the true vine, and my Father is the vinegrower."
John 15:1   5th Sunday of Easter, Cycle B

Think About It-

Scripture is filled with examples of religious imagination. In fact, Jesus often taught his message by using nontraditional images to explain concepts or traditions that people might otherwise not understand. Jesus uses the image of the vine and branches to symbolize our relationship to him. In *Luke 14:15–24* Jesus uses the image of a great banquet as a way to convey how God welcomes us all into his kingdom.

Choose one of the following Catholic symbols that you experience in your life and explain what it might symbolize: a **candle**, **holy water**, **music**, the **sign of peace**, **ashes**, **chrism**, the **Advent wreath**, the **crucifix**, a **statue of a saint**.

_____

_____

_____

_____

_____

_____

_____

Skill Steps-

The skill of Using Religious Imagination is like a muscle. We have it, but we don't always use it. However, the more often we use it, the better we become. This in turn will help strengthen our faith.

A religion teacher once asked a group of students to describe one of their favorite Catholic symbols. One student said, "Incense." When the teacher asked why, the student replied, "Because it reminds me that you pray best after you get burned." For this student, incense is a symbol that reminds him or her that we don't pray with words as much as with our hearts.

Exercise your religious imagination by choosing two Catholic gestures from the list. Describe what each signifies for you.

kneeling during Mass
making the Sign of the Cross
burning incense in church

dipping your finger in holy water
covering the cross on Good Friday
wearing a cross as jewelry

Explain your choices.

_____

_____

Check It Out-

Place a check mark next to the sentences that apply to you.

◯ I experience God's presence in everyday situations.

◯ I use my religious imagination when I pray.

◯ I see the opportunity to use my religious imagination at home.

◯ I experience my Catholic faith through people and relationships as well as objects.

How many did you check? Based on your response, what things do you need to work on?

_____

Closing Prayer-

Lord, you reveal yourself to us in so many ways. The majestic heights of the mountains, the pounding surf of the ocean, the fragile beauty of a bird's feather, the poetry of the psalms, and the prayers and rituals of your Church all help us experience your love for us. Thank you for continually giving us signs of your presence. Thank you for loving us so much that you are always willing to act in our lives.

Moments of Grace

Almighty God, throughout the ages you have cared for your people, leading and guiding us, patiently supporting us when we are troubled, lonely, uncertain, or frightened. We know you are always with us. Thank you for your love.

CHAPTER 2

14

Draw a symbol or create an image that represents a situation when someone helped you and another symbol or image that represents a situation when you helped someone.

Getting a
Helping Hand

There are times when each of us needs help and guidance. Family members, friends, teachers, and coaches may be sources of strength and wisdom for us. We may depend on another's humor, kindness, patience, or experience to help us find our way. We can accomplish far more and are more likely to be successful in overcoming obstacles in our lives if we can learn from others and depend on them for help.

Each of us should also look for opportunities to return the favor. We have talents and characteristics that others admire and need, and we can share them with those around us. By depending on one another, we can learn to deal with the problems we face every day. Loving relationships are built on giving and receiving.

God's Amazing Grace

The well-known hymn "Amazing Grace" was written by John Newton between 1760 and 1770 to express the wonderful gift of God's grace. A former captain of an English slave ship, Newton displayed no faith in God until he prayed during a terrible storm in 1748. Surviving the storm, Newton turned away from his former life and became a minister in the Church of England, preaching and writing hymns. Newton turned from a life of ignoring God to a life of experiencing God's grace and proclaiming it. Here is a verse from "Amazing Grace" that describes Newton's experience:

> Through many dangers, toils and snares,
> I have already come;
> 'Tis grace hath brought me safe thus far,
> And grace will lead me home.

For more information: Find the music and lyrics to "Amazing Grace." You may also wish to research the life of John Newton, using a biography of his life.

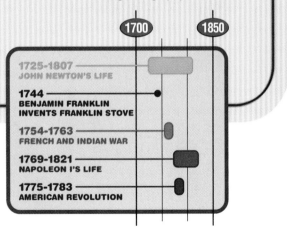

1700   1850

1725-1807
JOHN NEWTON'S LIFE

1744
BENJAMIN FRANKLIN
INVENTS FRANKLIN STOVE

1754-1763
FRENCH AND INDIAN WAR

1769-1821
NAPOLEON I'S LIFE

1775-1783
AMERICAN REVOLUTION

The Grace of God

Grace can have a profound effect on our lives. Have you ever faced a difficult challenge and wondered where the strength to do the right thing came from? This may have been God's grace at work in your life. Grace is God's free gift of himself that helps us overcome the challenges we face every day. For example, you have the opportunity to cheat on a test. Do you do it? Someone at school tries to draw you into a fight. Do you allow yourself to be drawn in, or do you walk away? When we accept God's grace in our lives, we respond to God's love, change our hearts, and are able to make morally right choices. You know that cheating on the test is wrong, so you choose not to do it. You know that the best thing for everyone involved is for you to control your anger and walk away from the fight, so you do. Through grace, God helps us value virtue and goodness.

Counting
on Christ

Our faith in Jesus Christ is the source of our lives as Christians. We believe that Jesus suffered, died, and was raised from the dead so that we might be saved from the power of sin and everlasting death. Catholics call this saving mystery the **Paschal mystery.** The sacraments unite us with Christ's Paschal mystery, and we celebrate God's saving actions in the world. In each of the sacraments, we die to our old selves. Then we rise to new life in God's grace, guided by the Holy Spirit to love and serve as Jesus did.

We experience the effects of grace in our lives all the time, even though we may not recognize them. Have you ever had an experience when someone did an unexpected favor for you? Maybe you were losing a board or video game and someone gave you an extra turn just so you could catch up. Maybe someone called you when you were feeling lonely and asked you to go to a movie. Generosity, joy, and honesty from people around us point to God's grace at work in our lives. Through God's grace we are strengthened to live responsibly and wisely.

Share with your Faith Partner an experience of grace.

FaiTH
ParTNeRSHiP

Opening the Word

Easter Tuesday

When she had said this, she turned around and saw Jesus standing there, but she did not know that it was Jesus. Jesus said to her, "Woman, why are you weeping? Whom are you looking for?" John 20:14–15

Read *John 20:11–18* as well as *Acts 2:22–36* and *Colossians 1:15–20.* What do these passages tell us about the Paschal mystery?

_____

_____

_____

_____

In the sacraments we are united with Christ and become members of his Body, the Church, which continues his work in the world. Our sins are forgiven, and the Holy Spirit strengthens us so that we can live our faith and witness to the saving power we have experienced in our lives. The sacraments help us deepen our faith and live as disciples of Jesus.

The writer of the Acts of the Apostles gives us many examples of the early Christians experiencing the Holy Spirit. Peter, for example, was a frightened man, unsure of himself and his faith in Jesus; the night before the crucifixion, he denied knowing Jesus. But the Spirit strengthened and guided Peter, and soon Peter was bravely teaching others about Jesus. (See *Acts 2:14–42.*) Through our participation in the sacraments, the Spirit strengthens us, too.

The Liturgical Year

Through the seasons and holy days of the **liturgical year,** the Church celebrates Jesus' passion, death, resurrection, and ascension—the Paschal mystery.

The liturgical year is different from the calendar year with which we are familiar.

The liturgical year begins with the Season of Advent, the first Sunday of which occurs in late November or early December. During Advent we recall the first coming of the Son of God into human history, and we prepare for the coming of Christ, in our hearts, in history, and at the end of time. Some families use an Advent calendar to mark the days before Christmas, or they might have a Jesse tree that recalls the many holy people who prepared the way for Jesus. Churches usually use an Advent wreath, something you may also have in your home. Lighting the candles of the wreath and praying and singing together help us prepare for Christmas. The liturgical color for Advent is violet.

The color for Christmas is white. (Any time white is used, gold may be used.) On Christmas we celebrate the Incarnation, the Son of God becoming one of us.

Catholics Believe

Grace is participation in the life of God. See Catechism, #1997.

How does participating in the life of God change you?

_____

_____

_____

_____

Lent is the season of prayer and sacrifice that begins with Ash Wednesday and lasts about forty days. Lent has always been a time of repentance through prayer, fasting, and almsgiving. During Lent we may spend more time in private prayer or participate in the Stations of the Cross or communal penance services. In remembering Jesus' willing sacrifice for us, we may decide to give up eating a favorite food. And we can try to be more generous, perhaps devoting time to helping with community projects. In Lent we prepare for Easter by examining our lives and finding ways to follow Jesus more closely by preparing for or renewing our conversion and Baptism. The liturgical color for Lent is purple.

Easter is the high point of the liturgical year because it celebrates Jesus' resurrection from the dead. The week beginning with Palm Sunday is called Holy Week. Lent ends on Holy Thursday evening, and the Easter Triduum begins. The Triduum, or three holy days, includes the observance of Holy Thursday (white), Good Friday (red), and the Easter Vigil on Holy Saturday (white).

In many wonderful ways our Church celebrations, especially during the Easter Season, express our joy in experiencing new life in Christ. As at Christmas, we use the color white during the Easter Season. This season lasts about seven weeks (fifty days) until Pentecost. At Pentecost, we celebrate the gift of the Holy Spirit sent to the followers of Jesus gathered in the upper room in Jerusalem.

Media Message

THE FAITHFUL MEDIA? Church is not the only place we hear about religion and our spiritual lives. We can also get messages about God and spirituality in the media: through the movies and television shows we watch, the songs we listen to, the magazines we read, the video games we play, and the Internet sites we visit. The messages may be about reincarnation, supernatural powers, angels, and beliefs about how God acts or doesn't act in our lives.

How has the media affected your understanding of your relationship with God? How do you decide what is hurtful and what is helpful?

_____

_____

_____

_____

_____

The liturgical color for Pentecost is red, a color that is also used during the celebration of the Sacrament of Confirmation because of that sacrament's connection with the Holy Spirit.

The majority of the liturgical year is called Ordinary Time. In this case the term *ordinary* means "ordered" (like "ordinal numbers") or "numbered" rather than "common." Ordinary Time is the time during the Church year that is not part of the Advent, Christmas, Lent, or Easter Seasons. During Ordinary Time the Church community reflects on what it means to walk in the footsteps of Jesus—to be his disciples. The liturgical color for Ordinary Time is green.

During the liturgical year we celebrate and commemorate Jesus' life and grow in discipleship. The liturgical year is the framework for the members of the Body of Christ to come together for prayer and liturgical celebrations.

Growing in **Grace**

The sacraments are celebrations of the Paschal mystery, enabling us to experience Christ's presence with us. They confer the grace of which they are a sign because Christ is at work in them. By celebrating the suffering, death, and resurrection of the Son of God, Jesus Christ, we enter more deeply into the life of faith to which we are called. The grace of the sacraments helps us respond to God with love and to love ourselves and others.

Think about how you get along with others. Is there a difficult person in your life who is very demanding and critical? Or maybe there is someone who is never happy and lets everyone know it. The grace of the sacraments can help you do what you know is right, such as be patient. You may not be able to make an unhappy person happy, but you may be able to put up with this person's unhappiness and not let it ruin your day or make his or her day worse. You may even find yourself able to appreciate some of this person's better characteristics!

When we meet God in the sacraments, we experience the power of his love. It is as if a close friend is always with us to support and guide us. We feel less selfish and more giving toward others. Our viewpoint gradually widens from thinking primarily about ourselves to thinking about God and other people.

Reflect on how the sacraments allow us to better understand our relationship with God. Share your thoughts with your Faith Partner.

WRAP UP

- The Paschal mystery refers to the suffering, death, and resurrection of Christ through which he saved us from the power of sin and everlasting death.

- Grace is God's life in us and the help we are given by the Holy Spirit to deepen our relationship with God.

- We celebrate the Paschal mystery through the sacraments and through the seasons of the liturgical year.

- In the sacraments we celebrate our lives as members of the Body of Christ.

What questions do you have about the content of this chapter?

_____

_____

_____

Around the Group

Discuss the following question as a group.

What are some moments of grace for Christians?

After everyone has had a chance to share his or her responses, come up with a group answer upon which everyone can agree.

_____

_____

_____

_____

What personal observations do you have about the group discussion and answer?

_____

_____

_____

_____

_____

Briefly...

At the beginning of this chapter, you were asked to recall an instance when you helped someone and when someone helped you. Based on what you have learned in this chapter, when have you felt aware of God's help, or when did you experience a moment of grace?

_____

_____

_____

Using Religious Imagination

Expressions of Faith-

The skill of Using Religious Imagination can help us sense moments of grace in our lives, thereby helping us experience God's love. When we use our religious imagination, we are not limited to objects or images we can paint or sculpt. We also use our religious imagination any time we experience the presence of God in an action or event.

> ### Scripture
>
> But immediately Jesus spoke to them and said, "Take heart, it is I; do not be afraid." Peter answered him, "Lord, if it is you, command me to come to you on the water." He said, "Come." So Peter got out of the boat, started walking on the water, and came toward Jesus.
>
> **Matthew 14:27–29**   19th Sunday of Ordinary Time, Cycle A

Skill Steps-

Recall what religious imagination is: the skill that can inspire us and open us to God's love in our lives. Religious imagination means using language, symbols, and gestures to express our relationship with God.

Here are some key points to remember:

- Jesus used religious imagination.
- Each of us has the ability and the obligation to use our religious imagination.
- We use language, symbols, and gestures to express our faith.
- We know God through the signs and symbols he uses to reveal himself to us.
- In Scripture the writers used religious imagination to communicate their experiences of God.
- We can use our religious imagination to motivate ourselves, renew our spirits, and grow in faith.

Skill Builder-

Exercise religious imagination by thinking of the following situations as opportunities for new beginnings. What symbol might you use for each?

Share your responses and thoughts with your Faith Partner.

○ A best friend moves away.

_____

○ An older brother or sister goes to college.

_____

○ You begin attending a new school.

_____

Putting It into Practice-

Now use your religious imagination to express your experience of God's grace in your life.

○ Describe a moment in your life when you had an experience of God that moved you deeply.

_____

_____

○ Through a poem, express the feeling of being protected or empowered by God.

_____

_____

Now that you have had some practice using your religious imagination, give yourself a letter grade. _____ Explain why you graded yourself the way you did. List one area in which you need to improve.

_____

Closing Prayer-

*God of power and mercy, you are always there for us. When we are hurt and angry, you **send** us comfort. When we are facing a tough challenge, you give us strength. When we are not sure what to do, you **grant** us wisdom. Where would we be without you? Our hearts are grateful that we can depend on you. In Jesus' name, we pray. Amen.*

Baptism

Father of us all, bless those who seek the waters of Baptism for new life in Jesus Christ your Son. And bless those of us who have already been baptized, that we may respond to your love and live as the Holy Spirit guides us.

What Do You Think?

List the groups you have chosen to join.
What were your reasons for joining each of these groups?

Group

_____

Reasons for joining

_____

_____

Group

_____

Reasons for joining

_____

_____

Group

_____

Reasons for joining

_____

_____

Group

_____

Reasons for joining

_____

_____

Group

_____

Reasons for joining

_____

_____

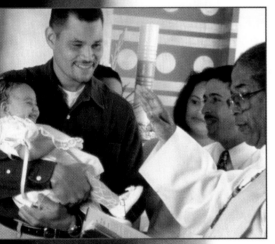

Be a
Part of It!

Think about why you belong to various groups.
Sometimes the association is automatic, as it is
with your family. But when you decide to join
a group, you may have to prepare in some way
before being admitted. This preparation, or
initiation, helps you know more about the group,
and it also helps the group know more about
you. To join the school band, for instance, you
must learn to play a musical instrument and
practice the music the band plays.

Joining a group means becoming part
of a new community. The way we look at
and experience life changes. The experience of gaining membership in a group
is similar to what happens in Baptism, the
first Sacrament of Christian Initiation. Becoming members
of the Church can bring out the best in us and help us
become the people God wants us to be.

Becoming a Christian

Who is your best friend? Why are the two of you so close? Is it because you share interests and participate in many activities together? Is it because you have come to know each other so well? Best friends are important. Good friends defend us and support us during difficult times.

Our relationship with Jesus is like that. We recognize all that he has done for us through his life, death, and resurrection. Believing in him, we want to be closer to him. We are fully initiated into the Church, the Body of Christ, through the Sacraments of Christian Initiation: Baptism, Confirmation, and Eucharist.

Opening the Word

Sunday After Epiphany, Cycle A

And when Jesus had been baptized, just as he came up from the water, suddenly the heavens were opened to him and he saw the Spirit of God descending like a dove and alighting on him. Matthew 3:16

Read *Matthew 3:13–17* as well as *Acts 2:38* and *Romans 6:1–4.* **What do these passages tell us about Baptism?**

_____

_____

_____

The Rite of Baptism

Baptism is the first sacrament. It is the beginning of our life in Christ. Most of the baptized people you know were probably baptized as infants. But Baptism can also be celebrated when an older child or adult chooses to become a Christian. As members of the Body of Christ, we welcome new members of all ages.

Baptism is celebrated in two ways in the Latin Rite of the Catholic Church—either separately as a sacrament for infants and young children or together with Eucharist and Confirmation for older children and adults. If you were baptized as an infant, you probably celebrated your First Communion in elementary school, and if you haven't celebrated Confirmation, you may be preparing for it.

Adults and older children go through the *Rite of Christian Initiation of Adults (RCIA).* In RCIA the person seeking initiation is older than seven, the age at which, according to the Church, a person can tell right from wrong. After the pre-catechumenate, a time of inquiry, the inquirer is welcomed into the catechumenate. The **catechumen,** or the person preparing for Baptism, states publicly his or her intention to become a member of the Church. The person then studies for a period of time, after which the Rite of Election or Enrollment of Names is celebrated, usually on the first Sunday of Lent. During this ceremony the Church formally acknowledges the catechumen's readiness for initiation. Lent is the time of reflection and final preparation. Then, often as part of the Easter Vigil, the elect are initiated into the Church through the celebration of the Sacraments of Baptism, Confirmation, and the Eucharist.

However Baptism is celebrated, we join the community in welcoming the individual into our Church family. If you have younger family members, you probably watch out for them and guide them. The same is true of our Church family. As members of the Body of Christ, we have a duty to help younger or less experienced members learn about and live our faith.

When infants and children are baptized, **godparents** have a special role in the celebration. They promise to help the newly baptized person grow in faith, and they join with parents in making this promise.

Share your ideas about the role of godparents with your Faith Partner.

FaiTH ParTNeRSHiP

Our Christian Journey

Initiation: Then and Now In the early centuries of the Church, many people became members of the Church as adults, although infants were also baptized. Adult catechumens studied, prayed, and prepared for their initiation for months or even years. Lent, the time during which the Church prepares for Easter, was the period of their final preparation. Then, during the Easter Vigil, which takes place during the hours preceding the dawn of Easter Sunday, the catechumens were baptized, confirmed, and received the Eucharist for the first time. Over the centuries this practice gradually came to an end. However, it was reinstituted after the Second Vatican Council in the form of the *Rite of Christian Initiation of Adults* (RCIA). Today our practice is similar to that of the early Church.

For more information: Speak to someone in your parish about how people can join the Church, or read your diocesan paper to learn about RCIA in your diocese.

Celebrating the Sacrament

The Sacrament of Baptism is often celebrated during Mass. The celebrant calls the family or families to the altar and welcomes all who are gathered for the celebration. The priest or deacon then blesses the baptismal water, after which the celebrant asks the person being baptized (or the parents and godparents in the case of an infant) a series of questions. These *baptismal promises* summarize key Christian beliefs. In making these promises, the person professes that he or she shares the beliefs of the community. Because we are members of Christ's Body, the Church, we renew our baptismal promises as the person being baptized first does so.

Next, the celebrant invites each family to the baptismal font for the Baptism. The one being baptized is then immersed in a pool of water or has water sprinkled or poured on him or her. Water is a sign of both life and death—death to one's old life and rebirth to a new life in Christ.

Through the waters of Baptism, we are cleansed of **original sin**—the first humans' choice to disobey God and the condition that each of us inherits. We are also strengthened to live holy lives as disciples of Christ. Water and the words of Baptism—"I baptize you in the name of the Father and of the Son and of the Holy Spirit"—are the essential signs of Baptism.

After the Baptism with water, the celebrant **anoints** the child or adult with oil. In the Bible kings and prophets were anointed to mark them as God's chosen people. Similarly, we are anointed with **chrism,** a sacred oil made from olive oil scented with spices, as a sign that we are set apart for Christ.

Next, the baptized person puts on or is dressed in a white garment to symbolize his or her new life in Christ. Finally, a candle is lit from the Paschal candle as a sign that the baptized person has been enlightened by Christ and is now a light to the world.

Catholics Believe

Baptism is the basis of Christian life: we are freed from sin and reborn in Christ; we become members of the Body of Christ. See Catechism, #1213.

Choose one of the symbols of Baptism and describe how it holds meaning for you and how it can remind you of your Baptism.

_____

_____

_____

Living Our Promises

With these signs and symbols, we prepare to live our lives in the Spirit. In fact, through the Sacrament of Baptism, we are marked by the Holy Spirit with a **sacramental character.** This character permanently marks us as members of Christ's Body and calls us to live in love and holiness as Jesus did.

Keeping our baptismal promises and accepting the grace of the sacrament will show in our personal lives. For example, we will try to live honestly and generously. We will do schoolwork and chores to the best of our ability. We won't lie or cheat. We will avoid self-destructive behaviors and exploitation of the environment and work to improve the lives of others rather than harming them physically, emotionally, or spiritually. No doubt this way of life will be difficult at times. But God doesn't demand perfection from us, just our very best. Making the right choices means living honestly and morally. It means living our baptismal promises.

Through Baptism we share in Christ's ministry. For example, when we develop our prayer life and celebrate the sacraments, we share in Jesus' priesthood. As members of the Body of Christ, we join in Jesus' role of prophet by supporting and living the Church's teachings on morality and justice. And finally, we use the gifts of wisdom and forgiveness in our treatment of others, and we take responsibility for our choices and behavior. In doing so, we imitate the kingly role that Jesus demonstrated for us.

Once initiated into the Body of Christ, we are no longer the same. We are reborn in Christ. Now we live not only for ourselves but for others, as Jesus did. We celebrate God's love and give him thanks.

When we serve others, set aside our differences with one another, and live in the Spirit with love, joy, peace, kindness, goodness, and faithfulness, we participate in the life of the Body of Christ.

Rite Response

The Water of Baptism

Water is an essential symbol in the Sacrament of Baptism. During the ceremony the celebrant asks God to bless the baptismal water so that those who are baptized in it "may be washed clean of sin and be born again" to live as children of God.

In the Body of Christ

Do you believe in God, the Father Almighty?

When we are baptized, we become members of the Body of Christ. Called to follow Jesus, we rely on the Holy Spirit to help us do what is right even when the right choice is difficult. The choices we make can bring us closer to God and keep as our most important focus our relationship with him.

We live our faith in the ordinary events of our lives. The Holy Spirit is with us to guide us whenever we need help and support. For example, perhaps you have a friend who is abusing alcohol or drugs. You realize that your friend is heading for serious trouble. You can rely on the Holy Spirit for the courage to face your friend and tell him or her that the drinking or drug abuse has to stop. You can support your friend while he or she gets help. Courage to confront your friend in this way shows real concern for him or her as well as respect for your friendship. This gift of the Spirit builds honesty and compassion in our relationships with others.

Being a member of the Body of Christ means that we are part of a community. This community, the Church, celebrates the sacraments and worships together. Baptism brings us into this community, and we live our relationship with God in the Church. We depend on and help the other members of the Body of Christ so that all of us together live in the light of God's love and extend that love to those who have not yet experienced it. We have been reborn to a new life to honor Christ and serve others.

Make a poster showing what it means to be a member of the Body of Christ. Share your thoughts with your Faith Partner.

FaiTH PaRTNeRSHiP

WRAP UP

- Through the Sacraments of Christian Initiation, Christ transforms us with new life in him.
- In Baptism our sins are forgiven, we are made members of the Body of Christ, and we are saved from the power of sin and everlasting death.
- The waters of Baptism cleanse us of original sin.
- Water and the words of Baptism are the signs of our rebirth to a new life in Christ.

What questions do you have about this chapter?

_____

_____

_____

Do you believe in
Jesus Christ, his only Son?

DO YOU REJECT SIN?

This is our faith.

Do you believe in
the Holy Spirit?

Do...

Around the Group

Discuss the following question as a group.

What are some ways you can share in Christ's mission as priest, prophet, and king?

After everyone has had a chance to share his or her responses, come up with a group answer upon which everyone can agree.

_____
_____
_____
_____

What personal observations do you have about the group discussion and answer?

_____
_____
_____
_____

Briefly...

At the beginning of this chapter, you were asked about the reasons you had for joining some of the groups to which you belong. If you were choosing to be baptized now, what reasons would you give for your choice?

_____
_____

Being Accountable

Expressions of Faith-

Because we have been baptized, we are members of the Body of Christ. This means we help one another live holy lives. We are accountable to one another for our thoughts, words, and actions. We are expected to base our decisions on our Christian values.

Scripture

Owe no one anything, except to love one another; for the one who loves another has fulfilled the law. The commandments . . . are summed up in this word, "Love your neighbor as yourself."

Romans 13:8–9   23rd Sunday of Ordinary Time, Cycle A

Think About It-

Every day people make demands of us. We have chores to do. We have homework. We are expected to show up at a certain time and place. Sometimes we can meet these demands. Other times it seems impossible. Being accountable requires us to do our best to make sure that we act responsibly and that our behavior is based on Jesus' teachings.

Being part of a community of faith, the Body of Christ, we have people we can turn to when we need help in choosing to live as baptized Christians.

Identify persons of virtue who fit the following characteristics— **a truthful person, an unselfish person, a prayerful person, a wise person, a loving person.** Place their names around the table.

a loving person

_____

a truthful person

_____

a wise person

_____

an unselfish person

_____

a prayerful person

_____

Skill Steps-

Think of two or three people you know and admire. Consider them your personal advisors. If you are faced with a tough decision, try imagining what their advice would be. Then act on it.

The key to using your personal advisors is to be honest about what you know each person would say. If you admire them for the right reasons, you will find God's grace and wisdom in their answers.

Now imagine that you are faced with one of the following situations. Circle one situation and describe the advice you think each of your personal advisors would give.

- You're at a friend's house after school, and he or she offers you a beer.
- Your younger sister needs help with her homework, but you promised a friend that you'd go to his soccer game.
- A friend confided in you that she is thinking about running away from home. She has asked you not to tell anyone.

Person 1: _____

Person 2: _____

Person 3: _____

Check It Out-

Place a check mark next to the sentences that apply to you.

○ I look out for others and try to act responsibly.

○ I try to base my behavior on Jesus' teachings.

○ I see many examples every day of ways to stay accountable.

○ I turn to my faith community for support and guidance.

○ I try to focus on what it means to live as a baptized member of the Body of Christ.

On a scale of 1 to 10 (1 being the easiest), how hard is it for you to practice this skill? _____

Closing Prayer-

Lord God, send the power of the Holy Spirit to us when we need encouragement and guidance. Through water and the Holy Spirit, you brought us to new life. As members of the Body of Christ, help us share your love with everyone we meet.

Confirmation

Come,
Holy Spirit,
awaken our
hearts to
God's love.
Come,
Holy Spirit,
make us wise
and gentle.
Come,
Holy Spirit,
strengthen us
to live as
we should.
Amen.

Place the name of a historical figure or a person you know and respect on the line next to the quality you think that figure or person represents.

trustworthy _____   supportive _____

courageous _____   honest _____

humble _____   respectful _____

generous _____   polite _____

cheerful _____   responsible _____

What characteristics do you admire about yourself?

_____

_____

_____

Taking a Stand

If someone you know is described as being responsible, what does this mean? It probably means that he or she speaks truthfully and can always be counted on. A responsible person doesn't try to mislead anyone and always does his or her best.

As Catholics we are called to live responsibly according to the values that Jesus taught us. Sometimes, though, it can be difficult to live as Jesus would want us to. Knowing we are part of a larger community of believers helps support and strengthen us to stand up for our beliefs even when we are on our own. The Sacrament of Confirmation, a Sacrament of Christian Initiation, seals us with the Spirit, which strengthens us in our faith. Confirmation enables each of us to live a virtuous and loving Christian life.

Strengthened in the Spirit

Young adults seem to have so much freedom. They stay out as late as they want. They make their own decisions about what to wear, what friends to spend time with, and what music to listen to. In wishing for that kind of freedom for ourselves, we often fail to realize the responsibility that comes with these choices. When we are older, we can't blame anyone else when we show up late for work. And although we can buy nonessential things, we first have to pay for such basics as housing, insurance, and medical care.

Opening the Word

Pentecost

When the day of Pentecost had come, they were all together in one place.... Divided tongues, as of fire, appeared among them, and a tongue rested on each of them. All of them were filled with the Holy Spirit. Acts 2:1, 3–4

Read *Acts 2:1–8* as well as *Luke 1:39–42, John 16:12–14,* and *1 Corinthians 2:9–13.* According to your reading, who is the Holy Spirit and what does the Spirit do?

_____
_____
_____
_____

As confirmed Catholics we are given more privileges, but we also have to be more responsible in sharing our talents and our faith. Through the Sacrament of Confirmation, another Sacrament of Christian Initiation, we are strengthened by the Holy Spirit to live with an awareness of our faith and the traditions of our Church.

In the Acts of the Apostles, we read that after Jesus ascended into heaven, the apostles met together on the Jewish Feast of Pentecost. This holiday was, and remains, the day when the Jewish people celebrate their covenant with God and the giving of the Torah, the books of the Law. (See *Exodus 34:10–11, 22.*) For Christians **Pentecost** is the day to celebrate the Holy Spirit descending upon the apostles, empowering them to bear witness in Jesus' name. The apostles gathered together because Jesus had just been crucified and they were afraid for their lives. Many of them were even afraid to admit they were followers of Jesus. But, strengthened by the Holy Spirit, the apostles received the courage to go out and live, preach, and baptize in Jesus' name. Through their words and actions, the fullness of the Holy Spirit overflowed in the new followers of Jesus as well. (See *Acts 2:1–4, 37–42.*)

Like the apostles we will often have questions about our faith. But also like them, we are called to celebrate and spread the gospel message to others. In Confirmation the **gifts of the Holy Spirit** are increased in us.

The Gifts of the **Holy Spirit**

To bear witness to Christ we must be strong, informed, and confident. So the Spirit helps us develop the gifts of *wisdom, understanding, counsel, courage (fortitude), knowledge, reverence (piety),* and *wonder and awe (fear of the Lord).*

Wisdom is a gift frequently associated with the Holy Spirit. In *2 Chronicles 1:10* King Solomon prays to God for the wisdom to be a good leader. For us, having wisdom means that we use common sense and that we see things with the eyes of faith.

The gift of *understanding* is closely related to wisdom. When we use the gift of understanding, we are aware of what is going on around us. We also recognize that certain actions will result in certain consequences. Understanding focuses on seeing the relationship between things.

Counsel is also called right judgment. In the same way that school counselors advise students, so we are often called on to advise others and to be open to advice ourselves. Good counsel involves taking the time to make a good decision after we consider the options and the consequences and praying for guidance.

Courage, or fortitude, is one of the gifts of the Holy Spirit that we associate most closely with the Sacrament of Confirmation. Courage is the strength of character that enables us to know what is right and to do what is right even when it would be easier to give in.

Knowledge helps us distinguish between truth and falsehood. Knowing the facts helps us avoid confusion and poor judgment. We gain knowledge by studying, but we also gain knowledge by trying to live as members of the Body of Christ.

Focus On

Symbols of the Spirit

There are several symbols for the Holy Spirit found in Scripture. At Jesus' baptism the Spirit came upon him in the form of a dove, and at Pentecost the Spirit came down upon the apostles like tongues of fire, or flames, and a great wind. (See *Matthew 3:16* and *Acts 2:2–3.*)

Witness to the Spirit

Thomas Merton was a Trappist monk who spent most of his life in a religious community near Bardstown, Kentucky. Though the Trappists emphasize silence, manual labor, and little or no traveling, Merton became known throughout the world for his writings on freedom, social justice, and spirituality. Philosophically, he insisted that we are not what we may superficially think ourselves to be. Merton also thought that we should neither avoid the world nor hide from it. Rather, through the power of the Spirit, we should be passionately involved in the world. Toward the end of his life, Merton became interested in what other religions, especially Buddhism, taught about holiness. While traveling in Asia to meet religious leaders, he died in Bangkok, Thailand.

For further information: Visit the official Web site of the Abbey of Gethsemani, where Merton was a monk, at *www.monks.org.* You may also wish to look in your library for books and movies about Merton's life.

Reverence, or piety, is the deep sense of love that helps us live as children of God and members of the Body of Christ. This gift means being faithful and devout. We celebrate the Eucharist often, pray and help others every day, and respect ourselves, our neighbors, the Church, and God. We are reverent toward all creation because it reflects God, whom we honor.

Wonder and awe, or the gift of fear of the Lord, is sometimes misunderstood to mean that we must be afraid of God. But our heavenly Father is a merciful God. Wonder and awe is our response to God who is holy, powerful, wise, beautiful, and almighty. We feel overwhelmed by the realization of all that God is, and we are flooded with thanks and praise for him.

When we celebrate the Sacrament of Confirmation, the Holy Spirit acts within us to nourish these gifts. Those preparing to celebrate the sacrament must be open to the Spirit's gifts, which will help them bear witness to their faith in Christ.

1900   **1975**

1915-1968
THOMAS MERTON'S LIFE

1939-1945
WORLD WAR II

1954-1968
CRUCIAL PERIOD IN THE
U.S. CIVIL RIGHTS MOVEMENT

1962
UGANDA BECOMES AN
INDEPENDENT STATE

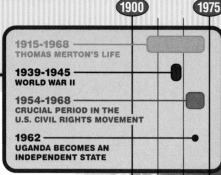

Becoming Witnesses

Confirmation continues our baptismal celebration. In fact, as part of the sacramental celebration, the candidates are asked to renew their baptismal promises. Like godparents in the Sacrament of Baptism, the **sponsor** of each candidate promises to help the candidate live his or her faith. Unlike Baptism, however, Confirmation is presided over in most cases by a bishop. As with all sacraments, God's word is proclaimed.

The two symbolic and essential actions during the ceremony are the **laying on of hands** and the anointing of the candidates' foreheads with chrism. During the anointing the one presiding says the words "Be sealed with the Gift of the Holy Spirit." The laying on of hands is an ancient practice found in the Bible. (See *Numbers 27:22–23* and *Acts 6:6, 8:17*.) With the laying on of hands, the outpouring of the Holy Spirit is invoked. The anointing with chrism on the forehead is the sign that the Holy Spirit brings us closer to Christ to be his witnesses and the sign that gives us the grace we need to live in Christ.

Through our celebration of the Sacrament of Confirmation, we are marked by the **Seal of the Holy Spirit,** which commissions us in Christ. Because the seal permanently changes us, the Sacrament of Confirmation, like the Sacrament of Baptism, can be celebrated only once.

Through the Sacrament of Confirmation, our relationship with God is deepened. We experience more completely that God is our loving Father and that we are his children. We also become more aware of the importance of Christ in our lives and are drawn more closely to him.

Further initiated into the Church community, we have a responsibility to be active members according to our age and abilities. As confirmed Christians we are given the strength and the courage to be witnesses for Christ and to reach out in word and action to bring others to him.

Discuss the responsibilities of a Confirmation sponsor with your Faith Partner.

Catholics Believe

The baptized are strengthened by the Holy Spirit through the Sacrament of Confirmation. See Catechism, #1285.

What gift of the Spirit do you need to strengthen your life? In what ways can this gift help you?

_____

_____

_____

Living Through the Spirit

Sealed with the Holy Spirit through Confirmation, we are called to live our faith with a deeper level of commitment than we had before we celebrated this sacrament. If we are open to the power of the Holy Spirit, our faith will not be something abstract and unfamiliar. We will live our lives as witnesses of Jesus' love and strength.

Faith will affect every decision and every action. If you meet someone who is having a bad day because he or she failed a test, don't hesitate to comfort that person. His or her feelings matter more than your "image."

If a teacher corrects your behavior in class, you might feel embarrassed at first, but try to understand that you were acting inappropriately. Instead of talking back, work on improving your future behavior. Respect your teacher's authority.

Our increased faith will also allow us to reconsider the importance of our family members. Instead of arguing with or feeling embarrassed by your family, try to understand them. Although you probably see them every day, how well do you really know them? What is your sister's favorite color? What is your mom's favorite song? The answers to these questions may seem insignificant, but they help you get to know more about the most important people in your life.

When we are responsible, respectful, and kind to others, we show them the love that Christ has for all of us. We bear witness to our faith.

Reflect on what it means to be sealed with the Spirit in Confirmation. Share your thoughts and responses with your Faith Partner.

FAITH PARTNERSHIP

WRAP UP

- Confirmation is a Sacrament of Christian Initiation.
- In Confirmation the Holy Spirit brings us closer to Christ.
- In Confirmation the Holy Spirit strengthens us, as the apostles were strengthened at Pentecost, to bear witness for Christ.
- Confirmation makes us more responsible for our faith.
- The gifts of the Holy Spirit are wisdom, understanding, counsel, courage, knowledge, reverence, and wonder and awe.

What questions do you have about this chapter?

_____

_____

_____

Around the Group

Discuss the following questions as a group.

In the United States, Confirmation is celebrated at different ages depending on the diocese: before First Communion, while in middle school, and while in high school. At what age does your diocese celebrate Confirmation? What are some good reasons to be confirmed at this age?

After everyone has had a chance to share his or her responses, come up with a group answer upon which everyone can agree.

_____

_____

_____

_____

What personal observations do you have about the group discussion and answer?

_____

_____

_____

_____

_____

Briefly...

At the beginning of this chapter, you were asked about the characteristics you admire in yourself. Which of these characteristics do you think are made stronger by celebrating the Sacrament of Confirmation?

Being Accountable

Expressions of Faith-

Along with the Eucharist, both Baptism and Confirmation are Sacraments of Christian Initiation—the sacraments by which we become ready to live Christ's call to us as members of his Body. When someone decides to celebrate the Sacrament of Confirmation, one thing he or she is doing is accepting the responsibility of being accountable to Christ in response to his call.

Scripture

I do not call you servants any longer, because the servant does not know what the master is doing; but I have called you friends, because I have made known to you everything that I have heard from my Father. You did not choose me but I chose you. And I appointed you to go and bear fruit. . . .

John 15:15–16   6th Sunday of Easter, Cycle B

Skill Steps-

There are two steps to being accountable. First, remember the values that Jesus taught us. Let his life be a model for your life. Second, remember to ask your imaginary advisors. Think of the people around you who represent the people of God and who act with love, respect, and concern for others. How might they react?
   Here are some key points to remember:

● You are accountable because of your Baptism.
● When you are accountable, you remain spiritually strong.
● Your behavior should be based on Jesus' teachings.
● The commandment to love your neighbor can help you make good decisions.

Skill Builder-

Imagine you are advising friends who are faced with the following situations.

◯ Instead of collecting information on the Internet for his class project, Michael is surfing white-supremacist sites.

_____

_____

◯ Tanya is planning to have a party when her parents are not home. Her friends want to bring alcohol to the party.

_____

_____

Putting It into Practice-

Now complete the following activity to practice being accountable.

⊙ List five people whom you respect to be your imaginary advisors. Include Jesus as one member of the group.

1. _____   4. _____

2. _____   5. _____

3. _____

⊙ What is an important decision that you recently made or that you will soon have to make?

_____

⊙ What kind of advice do you think each person would provide?

1. _____

2. _____

3. _____

4. _____

5. _____

Using what you have learned about the skill of Being Accountable, take time each day to put it into practice. Before you make a decision, do the following:

⊙ Remember to think of at least two possible actions you could take.

⊙ Imagine the consequences of what might happen in each case.

⊙ Remember to use Jesus and your other imaginary advisors to think about possible solutions.

Based on your experience with the skill so far, which of these steps of being accountable is easiest for you? Which of them requires more work?

_____

_____

Closing Prayer-

Father, send us your Spirit to help us follow your Son. May the Holy Spirit dwell in us to guide us and help us. May the Spirit turn our fears to courage, our weakness to strength, and our selfishness to generosity. May the Holy Spirit inspire us as the apostles were inspired at Pentecost. Amen.

CHAPTER 5

Eucharist

Almighty God, you always remember us, taking care of our every need. Whether we are strong or weak, troubled or happy, fearful or brave, you look out for us and watch over us. We turn to you with thanks and love. Through Christ our Lord. Amen.

List three things that are valuable to you and explain why you consider them valuable.

1. _____ _____
2. _____ _____
3. _____ _____

Name three people for whom you are thankful and explain why.

1. _____ _____
2. _____ _____
3. _____ _____

Describe a situation in which someone went out of his or her way to be generous to you. How did you thank him or her?

_____
_____
_____
_____

Giving Thanks

Think of a time when you felt thankful. Maybe your team won an important game, or a friend helped you through a tough time.

When we are thankful to someone, we are aware that our happiness is influenced by that person's action. We appreciate the fact that this person thought of us. When we have such an experience, we feel wonderful. We want to express our thanks and let him or her know how we feel.

Our relationship with God is like this. God constantly takes care of us and gives us gifts to bring us closer to him. To express our thanks, we celebrate the Eucharist, also called the Mass. We gather together as members of the Body of Christ, and we give thanks and praise to God for all that he does for us.

Symbolic Action

Several retellings of the Last Supper appear in the New Testament, each with its own focus. In fact, no two are exactly the same.

In the Gospels, the Last Supper takes place around the time of **Passover,** the Jewish feast celebrating the delivery of the Israelites from slavery in Egypt. But the author of the Gospel according to John structures the story to make an important point. Because the Last Supper occurs in John's Gospel on the day before Passover, Jesus' crucifixion—which occurred the day after the Last Supper—would have taken place on Passover. The readers of John's Gospel, therefore, would have compared Jesus' sacrifice with the sacrificial lamb the Jews slaughtered on Passover. Jesus' saving action would become the new and perfect Passover lamb.

Opening the Word

Corpus Christi, Cycle B

While they were eating, he took a loaf of bread, and after blessing it he broke it, gave it to them, and said, "Take; this is my body." Mark 14:22

Read *Mark 14:22–26* as well as *Matthew 26:17–30*, *John 6:30–38*, and *1 Corinthians 11:17–34*. What do these passages tell us about Eucharist?

_____

_____

_____

Our Celebration of Thanks

In biblical times meals were symbolic: they celebrated God's ability to provide for his children and thanked him for his saving presence. The breaking of bread signified unity and reconciliation. When people came together to "break bread," they celebrated a bond of family unity or friendship.

When we gather for the Sacrament of the Eucharist, we celebrate in the same spirit. We acknowledge our thankfulness to God the Father and his Son through a community meal. In fact, the word **Eucharist** comes from a Greek word meaning "thanksgiving."

As with all the sacraments, the Eucharist celebrates the Paschal mystery. We recall and celebrate Jesus' suffering, death, and resurrection. We give thanks that Jesus brings us to his Father, and we celebrate the Holy Spirit, who acts in our lives to make us a holy people. Throughout the liturgical year we celebrate the Eucharist by worshiping together as members of the Body of Christ, dedicating ourselves to a Christian life.

At the Last Supper Jesus took bread, blessed it, broke it, and gave it to his disciples to eat. This happens again whenever we gather to celebrate the Eucharist. The priest, in the name of Jesus, takes the bread, blesses it, and gives it to us.

The Liturgy of the Word

Our celebration of the Eucharist begins with the *Introductory Rites.* We gather together singing a hymn, and the celebrant greets us. During the *Penitential Rite* that follows, we acknowledge our sins and praise God for his mercy. The priest then prays a prayer of forgiveness. Sometimes we pray or sing the *Glory to God.* The *Opening Prayer* relates to the theme of the mass.

The first great part of the Mass is called the **Liturgy of the Word.** During this liturgy we listen to the word of God in readings from the Old and New Testaments. Through Scripture God reveals himself to us and guides us to him. We respond to the first reading with a joyful psalm, or song from Scripture. After

the second reading and Alleluia verse, the celebrant proclaims the good news of Jesus' life and teachings as recounted in one of the four Gospels.

Next, the priest or deacon speaks to us about the readings we have heard. This is the *homily,* which helps us understand how we can apply the message of the readings to our lives. Then, we recite together the *Profession of Faith,* or declaration of our Christian beliefs. Finally, during the *General Intercessions,* we offer prayers for the needs of the community, the Church, and the world.

With your Faith Partner make a list of your community's needs.

FaiTH PaRTNeRSHiP

Rite Response

Objects Used at Mass

During the Mass we use special objects to help us celebrate. The *paten* is the plate that holds the *hosts,* or bread, that becomes the Body of Christ. The *chalice* is the cup that holds the wine that becomes the Blood of Christ. The *flagon* also holds wine. The *sacramentary* is the book that contains the prayers for the Mass. The *cruets* are the small containers, usually made of glass, that hold the wine and water used at Mass. The *ciborium,* or Eucharistic dish, is the covered container used to keep consecrated hosts. The ciborium is kept in the *tabernacle,* a special box-like receptacle. The *ambo* is the reading stand from which the Scripture is read and the homily is given.

Something to Celebrate The celebration of the Eucharist is the central event of the Church. Over the centuries many Church councils, or official meetings of bishops and Church advisors, have dealt with the topic of the Eucharist. The Council of Trent, one of the most important councils in the history of the Church, issued an important statement about the Eucharist. In this decree the Council fathers wished to affirm the official Church position that the bread and wine become the Body and Blood of Christ during the celebration of the sacrament. They used the word **transubstantiation** to explain that the bread and wine offered at Mass are actually changed in their substance to Christ's Body and Blood, even though they keep the appearance of bread and wine. Catholics, then, believe that Christ is truly present in the consecrated Bread and Wine. This is called the **Real Presence.**

For more information: Research Pius X and the changes he made regarding the reception of Communion. Ask a librarian for good sources, use a Catholic encyclopedia, or consult the Internet.

1450 **1575**

1451-1506
CHRISTOPHER COLUMBUS'S LIFE

1506-1552
SAINT FRANCIS XAVIER'S LIFE

1545-1563
COUNCIL OF TRENT

1549
JESUIT MISSION TO JAPAN

The Liturgy of
the Eucharist

The second great part of the Mass is called the **Liturgy of the Eucharist.** We begin this part of the celebration by bringing our offerings, including the bread and wine, to the altar. This is the *Preparation of the Gifts.* In the name of the community, the priest receives the gifts and prays over them.

During the *Eucharistic Prayer,* a prayer of thanksgiving, the priest gathers our prayers with the prayers of all the Church and asks God the Father to send the Spirit upon our gifts. He asks that by the power of the Holy Spirit, our gifts of bread and wine may become the Body and Blood of Christ. The priest, through the power of God, consecrates the bread and wine.

We call the Eucharist a *sacrifice,* something special done or given out of love, because Jesus lived and died to save us. Our celebration of the Eucharist is also a sacred meal because our heavenly Father gives us his only Son, who is the Bread of Life.

The next part of the Liturgy of the Eucharist is the *Communion Rite.* We pray together the Lord's Prayer and the Doxology, a prayer glorifying and praising the Trinity. Then, during Communion, we receive the Body and Blood of Christ. To recognize and experience hunger for this holy meal, the Church asks us not to eat or drink anything except water for one hour before Communion.

When we have received Communion, we once again thank God for his generosity. Finally, in the *Concluding Rite,* renewed in the Spirit, we pray the *Prayer After Communion,* and we are sent forth to live in Christ. We are called to spread his peace and justice throughout the world to become the Body of Christ for others.

The Fruits of Communion

The Eucharist is the source and summit of our Christian life. It is a celebration of the totality of our faith and the renewal of grace that comes to us through all the sacraments. The effects of the Eucharist are present in everything we do. Through the Eucharist we are nourished with the abundance of gratitude, love, joy, and hope that comes from full membership in the Body of Christ. We anticipate the heavenly banquet and the eternal happiness that will be ours.

When we participate in the Mass, we experience the saving love of Christ and the grace of God. We become more sensitive to those who are hurting and those who are in need. Because of Christ's example, we will work to change the structures of society that bring pain and suffering to people.

As part of our celebration of thanksgiving, we recognize that through the Eucharist our venial sins have been forgiven. And because of our renewed relationship with Christ, we are better able to avoid sin in the future. We are strengthened to make good moral decisions and to do works of justice and charity.

The Eucharist is a sign of the unity that ought to be present in the Church. It should lead us to pray and work for the union of Christian Churches. This may mean being tolerant of others' beliefs rather than criticizing them for being different.

Each time we gather for Eucharist, we celebrate our membership in the Body of Christ. The Eucharist is a time, place, and way in which we bring our lives to God as offering and thanksgiving. Through the grace of the Father, the example of his Son, and the power

of his Spirit, we receive the nourishment to continue to grow as the Body of Christ in the Eucharist. This sacrament is a celebration of what "has been" and what "can be" through faith and grace.

When we receive Communion, we receive Christ himself.
See Catechism, #1382.

What can you do to prepare yourself to receive Christ in Communion?

_____

_____

_____

A Eucharistic People

For us as Catholics the sacraments are the center and source of our life in Christ. Our relationship with Jesus is rooted in the sacraments, especially the Eucharist. Some of the sacraments, like Baptism and Confirmation, are celebrated only once in our lives. But the Sacrament of the Eucharist should be celebrated often. We participate in the life of the community and celebrate this sacred meal with the rest of the Church. The Eucharist plays a central role in our lives as Christians. This is why we are often called a Eucharistic people.

Think about your life. Do you consider yourself a Eucharistic person? Who or what inspires you to do good? Where do your beliefs and ideals come from? If Jesus is important to you, draw closer to him through the Eucharist. If someone encourages you to go against your principles, such as pressuring you to have sex or use drugs, how do you decide what to do? As a Catholic you can depend on your relationship with Jesus in the Eucharist to help you know what is right for you and to have the strength to see it through.

In the Eucharist Jesus offers himself to his Father out of love for us. Whenever we celebrate this sacrificial meal, our venial sins are forgiven and God's grace is strengthened within us. We experience the Real Presence of Jesus with us. We are renewed and nourished to live in Christ and to share his peace and love with everyone.

Reflect on the central role of the Eucharist in our lives. Share your thoughts with your Faith Partner.

FaiTH ParTNeRSHiP

WRAP UP

- The Eucharist is a Sacrament of Christian Initiation and the source and summit of our Christian life.
- The Eucharist is the sacrament of Jesus' presence with us.
- In the Eucharist we receive the Body and Blood of Christ.
- At Mass we gather together as the Church to give thanks and to praise God.
- Through the Eucharist we anticipate the heavenly banquet, eternal life in the fullness of the kingdom.

What questions do you have about this chapter?

_____

_____

_____

Around the Group

Discuss the following question as a group.

How can we live as Eucharistic people?

After everyone has had a chance to share his or her responses, come up with a group answer upon which everyone can agree.

_____

_____

_____

_____

What personal observations do you have about the group discussion and answer?

_____

_____

_____

_____

Briefly...

At the beginning of this chapter, you were asked to list things which you find valuable and people for whom you are thankful. How was your faith reflected in your response? Based on what you have learned in this chapter, do you want to add anything to your original response?

_____

_____

_____

Staying Hopeful

Expressions of Faith—

In the Sacrament of the Eucharist, we are reminded that we have every reason to be hopeful people. Yet it can be hard to stay hopeful every day.

We face troubles and anxieties that overshadow the promises God has made us. As Catholics we may know why we should be hopeful, but sometimes we don't know how to go about it. Often we need to use our faith to gain the courage to stay hopeful. Staying hopeful will help you live as one of Christ's followers.

Scripture

"Come to me, all you that are weary and are carrying heavy burdens, and I will give you rest. Take my yoke upon you, and learn from me; for I am gentle and humble in heart, and you will find rest for your souls. For my yoke is easy, and my burden is light."

Matthew 11:28–30

14th Sunday of Ordinary Time, Cycle A

Think About It—

No one is happy and enthusiastic every day. Sometimes we have good reasons for being unhappy or sad. Sometimes we just need a little practice being more optimistic and hopeful. Hopefulness is a feeling of looking forward to the future and believing that even though bad things happen, good things happen, too. In the following examples, place an abbreviation before each of the statements (Really True—RT, Somewhat True—ST, and Not True—NT).

_____ 1. Bad things tend to happen to me and those I care about.

_____ 2. I tend to give up easily.

_____ 3. I don't like taking on new tasks.

_____ 4. I usually don't make a good impression on new people I meet.

_____ 5. In general I'm a hopeful person.

_____ 6. God helps me when I need it.

_____ 7. If someone doesn't answer me when I say hello, I tend to think the person didn't hear me.

_____ 8. I can usually succeed at a new project.

Are you a hopeful person?
If you answered RT to 1–4, or NT to 5–8, you might have trouble staying hopeful. If you answered NT to 1–4, or RT to 5–8, you are probably a person who finds it easy to stay hopeful. Whatever your answers, you can decide that you will be a hopeful person.

Skill Steps

Sometimes we may feel so overwhelmed by our emotions and concerns that we are not sure what we are feeling. There is a simple way to handle any emotion that is so strong that it seems to be taking control. Remember three easy steps: name it, tame it, and claim it.

Name it means identifying exactly what you are thinking and feeling. *Tame it* means that you try to gain control over the emotion by admitting that you are experiencing it. Is this a permanent situation? Do I have the power to change it? Is this the way things frequently happen to me?

After you have *named it* and *tamed it,* then you can *claim it.* None of us are completely in control of everything that happens to us. We can, however, choose how we respond to things. The key is not to let our emotions control who we are and how we act.

How do you name, tame, and claim feelings of hopelessness?

Let's say you are feeling hopeless because you are having trouble in your English class.

- First, name it. Identify how you are feeling. "I feel stupid and way behind."
- Then, tame it. Ask yourself the three questions: Is this a permanent situation? "Not necessarily." Do I have the power to change it? "Yes, if I admit that I'm having trouble and ask for help." Is this the way things usually happen to me? "No, I usually do well in school."
- Finally, claim it. What can you do to learn from this? How can you put this experience or emotion to productive use? Maybe you can tell yourself not to give up so easily or not to wait so long before asking for help. Claiming a situation means finding a productive way to improve your situation while also looking to God and others for support and guidance.

Check It Out

Place a check mark next to one of the following responses.

When it comes to managing my emotions, which is the most difficult for me?

◯ Naming It

◯ Taming It

◯ Claiming It

What does this tell you about yourself?

_____

_____

Closing Prayer

God our Father, you call us to the Eucharistic banquet table to feed us and renew our hearts. We give thanks to you for your Son, Jesus Christ, who gave himself for us so that we could be close to you. May your Holy Spirit help us live every day with thanks and praise for your mercy and kindness. Amen.

CHAPTER 6

Reconciliation

Jesus, sometimes we hurt others by making wrong choices and acting selfishly. Forgive us, and help us choose what is right. Bring us to forgiveness and healing, and help us change our hearts.

Complete the following sentences to describe the experience of sin and our desire to make things right again.

When a friend lies to me, I feel _____
_____

If someone insults me out of anger, I _____
_____

If I want to apologize for something I did, I _____
_____

Describe a time when you did not want to reconcile with someone but are glad that you did it anyway.
_____
_____

The Loneliness of Sin

When you and your friends or family have a disagreement, how do you get over your anger and hurt? Do you apologize? Do you try to make up for the misunderstanding in some way?

Sin causes separation. It harms and sometimes destroys relationships and drives people apart. Because of sin, we distrust one another, and often we feel lonely and isolated. When we experience the separation and hurt caused by sin, God wants to act in our lives to heal us. He invites us to *reconcile,* or be brought back together, with him, with those we have hurt or who have hurt us, with the Church, and with ourselves. In turning toward God, we find ways to make amends for the wrongs we have done and to be forgiving of others.

The Sacrament of Reconciliation, one of the Sacraments of Healing, is also one of the sacraments through which God forgives sins. In this sacrament we celebrate God's mercy and forgiveness. With God's grace we are no longer separated. Instead, we are united in celebrating God's forgiveness and the peace it brings.

Recognizing
Our
Sinfulness

Sin hurts our relationship with God, self, and others. But through the Sacrament of Reconciliation, we celebrate God's forgiveness and learn to heal our relationships. If we recognize the pain we have caused and are sorry for our sinful thoughts or actions, we can be forgiven. We can learn from our poor choices and work to live more virtuous lives.

During a meal that Jesus attended in the house of a Pharisee, a woman whom people judged to be a sinner entered and approached Jesus. She washed his feet with her tears and dried them with her hair. She then kissed his feet and anointed them with oil. The Pharisee was surprised that Jesus allowed the woman to do this because she was known as a sinful person. But Jesus said that because the woman had shown great love, her sins were forgiven. (See *Luke 7:36–50.*)

Like the woman in the story, we are called to seek forgiveness and ask for God's mercy and grace in our lives. How do you know when you need to seek God's forgiveness? You know because sin is a deliberate choice you make. Perhaps you drink a beer at a friend's house, something you know is wrong (a sin of *commission*). Or perhaps you hear some hurtful gossip about someone and you know that the gossip is untrue, but you do nothing to stop it (a sin of *omission*).

God gives us the gift of **conscience,** the ability to tell right from wrong and to choose what is right. Because of our conscience, we know the difference between a sin and something that goes wrong by accident. As we develop a habit of choosing what is right, it becomes easier to do so.

Share with your Faith Partner your thoughts about how we develop our conscience.

FaiTH PaRTNeRSHiP

Catholics *Believe*

Jesus' call to conversion and penance means changing our hearts. This will lead to changing the way we act. See Catechism, #1430.

What do you think it means to "change our hearts"?

_____

_____

_____

Looking at Your Life

When we prepare for the Sacrament of Reconciliation, we look at how well we are living the Christian life. This is called an **examination of conscience,** a prayerful way of recognizing our strengths and weaknesses and admitting to the presence of sin in our life.

Venial sin, or less serious sin, weakens our relationship with Jesus and with other members of the Body of Christ. The Sacrament of Reconciliation helps us overcome the petty habits and selfishness that characterize venial sin and strengthens our union with Jesus. Even when sin is very serious, or *mortal* (such as murder), the Sacrament of Reconciliation is always available. A mortal sin breaks the bond with Christ and his Church completely. But anyone who is truly sorry and who seeks God's forgiveness can turn to this Sacrament of Healing.

Although you can examine your conscience at any time, anywhere, a quiet place and time are helpful. Before you start, pray to the Holy Spirit for guidance. Then ask yourself questions about your attitudes and actions as they affect your relationships with God, others, and self. You might use the Ten Commandments to review your decisions. For example, do I put God first in all things? Do I lie? Do I steal? The Beatitudes may also help you decide whether your attitudes and actions are truly Christian. Do you forgive easily? Do you try to find peaceful solutions to disagreements?

After you become used to reviewing your attitudes and actions, you will develop your own questions. You may refer to Scripture for help, or you may personalize your questions based on areas of your life that you know need work.

Our Christian Journey

Medieval Penitential Books While today we emphasize the forgiveness and healing of the Sacrament  of Reconciliation, people of earlier times focused on how to make up for their wrongdoing. Priests during the Middle Ages used special books, known as penitentials, when listening to confessions. These manuals listed specific penances for sins. The penances were based on the sin committed and the social rank of the sinner. Usually, a penance was the length of time a sinner had to fast, but a penance could also include reciting the psalms and other practices. The penitentials, written by priests and monks experienced in hearing confessions, were never official Church documents.

For further information: Research or talk to someone of a different faith about the role of reconciliation in other religions.

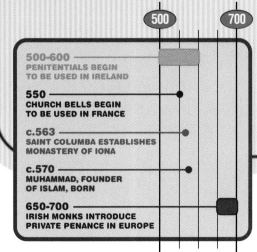

500   700

500-600
PENITENTIALS BEGIN
TO BE USED IN IRELAND

550
CHURCH BELLS BEGIN
TO BE USED IN FRANCE

c.563
SAINT COLUMBA ESTABLISHES
MONASTERY OF IONA

c.570
MUHAMMAD, FOUNDER
OF ISLAM, BORN

650-700
IRISH MONKS INTRODUCE
PRIVATE PENANCE IN EUROPE

Conversion

When we recognize and regret our sins, we begin the process of **conversion,** or turning back to God. In conversion we seek God's grace and rely on him with trust and hope. We know that he will help us become less self-centered and more attentive to the needs of others.

If we lie about going to a place our parents or guardians don't approve of, we can lose our family's trust and respect. As part of our conversion, we admit that our decision to go was wrong and that we lied to cover it up. Even though we admit our wrongdoing, we still must work to rebuild the trust that was broken.

When we are truly sorry for the wrongs we have done, we become more aware of the choices that led us to sin, and we can decide to change our behavior. Our sorrow, also called **contrition,** helps us grow in our relationships and in our faith. Contrition reminds us to love others as Jesus loves us all.

Media Message

VIDEO GAME VIOLENCE How do the media affect the good and bad choices we make? Do you think the media affect you at all? For example, some people say that violent video games encourage violence. Others say that violent video games can be a safe and healthy way to channel aggression or frustration. Still others say that violent video games become a problem only when the person playing them becomes obsessed with such games.

What do you think? Do violent video games make a person more likely to act violently in everyday life? Explain.

_____
_____
_____
_____

Celebrating the **Sacrament**

We can celebrate the Sacrament of Reconciliation individually or we may be part of a communal, or group, celebration. (In cases of grave necessity, a bishop may allow general confession and general absolution.) During the communal celebration, we may listen to Scripture readings and together reflect on an examination of conscience. In both forms of the sacrament, we confess our sins to a priest. Talking with a priest helps us see more clearly and take responsibility for our attitudes and actions. The priest then advises us about how we might avoid a particular pattern of sin. After we confess our sins, we pray an Act of Contrition, a prayer of sorrow. In the name of Christ and the Church, the priest offers us **absolution.** This prayer is an effective sign of God's forgiveness and of the grace he offers to help us live as Christians.

Although our sins are forgiven, forgiveness alone does not eliminate the pain and problems our sins can cause. So before the priest absolves us, he asks us to complete a **penance** to show we are serious about changing our lives. Usually a penance includes prayers or actions that help make up for the harm our sins have done. If we have stolen, we must return what we took or pay the owner back. If we lied, we must apologize and tell the truth. If we harmed another's reputation, we must take back our hurtful statements, admit our wrong, and work to rebuild trust with that person.

Focus On

Seal of the Sacrament

A priest is never allowed to tell anyone what he is told in confession. This is called the Seal of the Sacrament, and it guarantees that you can be open and honest in your confession, even if you did something illegal.

Opening the Word

7th Sunday of Ordinary Time, Cycle B

When Jesus saw their faith, he said to the paralytic, "Son, your sins are forgiven." Mark 2:5

Read *Mark 2:1–12* as well as *Matthew 18:21–22, Luke 15:11–32,* and *Luke 19:1–12.* What do these passages say about forgiveness?

_____

_____

_____

_____

A Chance **to Grow**

Reconciliation is our chance to make things right—to return to a life in union with God. Of course, facing up to our sins can be uncomfortable, but we should see beyond the initial discomfort. When we apologize to a friend for something we did, a true friend forgives us. Together we can continue a friendship that brings us happiness and love.

The same is true of our relationship with God. He has promised that if we are truly sorry for our sins, we will be forgiven. In turn, we are rewarded with stronger relationships with our friends and with God.

Growing in
Goodness

Jesus knew that we would need support and guidance to follow him. That is why he sent us the Holy Spirit and why we are made members of Christ's Body, the Church. Through the sacraments we celebrate together as the Church, especially Eucharist and Reconciliation, we are strengthened in our relationship with God. And his grace helps us resist temptations to sin and strengthens us in holiness.

Think of examples of virtuous people you know. What qualities do you admire in them? How do they show these qualities in their everyday lives? How might you imitate some of these qualities?

When you are shopping, the clerk gives you too much change. Instead of keeping the money, you return it. Or perhaps you have done something your parents or guardians asked you not to do. You know you can tell a convincing lie and avoid trouble, but instead of lying you tell the truth and accept the consequences. When you make these right choices, you are living honestly. Each day you have the opportunity to sin or to live virtuously.

Reflect on how you can live a virtuous life. Share your thoughts with your Faith Partner.

WRAP UP

- The Sacrament of Reconciliation is one of the Sacraments of Healing.

- When we sin, we hurt our relationship with God, self, and others.

- God has given us the gift of conscience—the ability to tell right from wrong and to choose what is right.

- We seek forgiveness for our sins in the Sacrament of Reconciliation.

- Through the Sacrament of Reconciliation, we are healed of the pain and separation that sin can cause, our sins are forgiven, and we are brought back into relationship with God and with others.

What questions do you have about this chapter?

_____

_____

_____

Around the Group

Discuss the following question as a group.

How is the Sacrament of Reconciliation a source of strength to live a better life?

After everyone has had a chance to share his or her responses, come up with a group answer upon which everyone can agree.

_____
_____
_____
_____

What personal observations do you have about the group discussion and answer?

_____
_____
_____
_____

Briefly...

At the beginning of this chapter, you were asked to describe the desire of making things right again. How has learning about Reconciliation, a Sacrament of Healing, changed your understanding of making things right?

_____
_____
_____
_____

Staying Hopeful

Expressions of Faith–

The Sacrament of Reconciliation celebrates forgiveness—God forgives our sins and heals us, reconciling us with himself, the Church, ourselves, and others. Knowing that God is willing to forgive us when we recognize what we have done wrong and are contrite restores our hope and strengthens us to live virtuously.

Scripture

Then he said to her, "Your sins are forgiven." But those who were at the table with him began to say among themselves, "Who is this who even forgives sins?" And he said to the woman, "Your faith has saved you; go in peace."

Luke 7:48–50   11th Sunday of Ordinary Time, Cycle C

Skill Steps–

Remember the steps for staying hopeful when you're feeling down. *Name It* by identifying what you are thinking and feeling. *Tame It* by finding a way to keep the emotion under control. *Claim It* by using the emotion in the most productive way.

Here are some key points to remember:

● We are a hopeful people because Christ has promised us eternal life.
● We can stay hopeful by recognizing that our emotions need not overwhelm us.
● Through the sacraments God acts in our everyday lives, giving us the strength and insight we need to work out our problems.

Skill Builder–

Practice staying hopeful by using the *Name It, Tame It, Claim It* strategy. For each of the following situations, imagine what you might feel and then use the strategy for staying hopeful.

Remember to consider questions such as the following to *Tame It. Is the situation permanent? Do you have the power to change it? Is this the way things usually happen in your life?* Then suggest ways you might be able to handle the situation to *Claim It*:

Name It: **I am failing math because I don't understand it.**

Tame It: _____

Claim It: _____

Name It: **My family is always criticizing me.**

Tame It: _____

Claim It: _____

Share your responses and thoughts with your Faith Partner.

FAITH PARTNERSHIP

Putting It into Practice-

Use the *Name It, Tame It, Claim It* strategy in your own life by thinking of a personal problem you are dealing with and working through the process by answering the questions below. Choose a situation that does not involve temptation or sin and is fairly typical of people your age.

⬤ Name It

The problem is _____

When I think about the problem, I hear myself thinking _____

_____

When I think about the problem, I feel _____

_____

⬤ Tame It

Is this problem permanent? _____

Do I have the power to change this problem? _____

Has this ever happened to me before? Does it happen to me frequently?

_____

⬤ Claim It

How can I use this experience in a productive way? _____

_____

What have I learned from this? _____

_____

As soon as you can identify the kinds of feelings that affect how you feel, you can work to change your behavior.

What aspects of staying hopeful are you good at?

_____

What things do you still need to work on?

_____

Closing Prayer-

*Lord, we are sorry for the wrong things we choose to do and the good things we choose not to do. When we sin, we turn away from you, the one who **loves us most**. Forgive us and help us open our hearts to your grace. Guide us in leading good lives and fill our hearts with your mercy. Heal us of all pain and sadness and give us hope. Amen.*

CHAPTER 7

Anointing
of the Sick

Holy Spirit, remember our friends and family members who are ill. Bring them strength and patience. Ease their pain and help them know that they are not alone.

Explore some of your attitudes and experiences of illness and death by checking *Yes* or *No* in response to the following statements.

Yes No

◯ ◯ I have had to go to the hospital when I was hurt or ill.

◯ ◯ Eventually medical science will cure all illnesses.

◯ ◯ I have experienced the death of someone close to me.

◯ ◯ Getting well is a matter of fixing the body.

◯ ◯ I don't like being around people who are ill.

◯ ◯ I have attended a wake or a funeral.

◯ ◯ People need to be healed spiritually as well as physically.

◯ ◯ I have visited someone in a hospital or other care center.

◯ ◯ I think I would enjoy caring for those who are ill or frail.

Describe your experience of facing either your own illness or that of someone else.

_____

_____

_____

Health and
Healing

When we are healthy, we may not think about our bodies much at all. But when we become ill, we may suddenly become aware of every movement and every twinge of pain.

You may not have directly experienced serious illness or the death of a loved one, but eventually you will face this part of life. Fortunately, medical science can do much to help us when we are ill or injured. But healing can be more than a physical experience. We celebrate the Sacrament of the Anointing of the Sick, a Sacrament of Healing, to help heal those with serious illnesses or those who are facing death because of illness, injury, or old age.

Jesus the **Healer**

Have you ever suffered some physical injury or been seriously ill? If so, you may have felt weak or helpless. You may have been angry because you couldn't do the things you normally enjoy. Perhaps you thought that the situation wasn't fair and that you shouldn't have had to go through it. These are all normal responses to suffering, even if the suffering isn't life threatening. The Church celebrates the Sacrament of the Anointing of the Sick to help us when we suffer or face the possibility of death.

The pain and hurt we experience from sin and its effects can be healed through celebrating the Sacrament of Reconciliation. But when we experience pain and hurt from illness, we also need God's mercy, comfort, and healing. Jesus knew that illness or dying affects the entire person, body and spirit. So when Jesus healed, he healed both body and spirit. He strengthened those who were ill by forgiving their sins as well as by making them physically healthy. He comforted them and gave them hope and trust in God.

Often Jesus asked those he was going to cure to have faith. He did not just mean that faith would cure illness but that we must trust in God no matter what happens. Jesus wants us to remember that God does not abandon us when we are at our weakest. Instead, he is the one we can turn to for support. Illness, like all other aspects of life, can become a means of conversion and can help lead us to God.

Opening the Word

4th Sunday of Lent, Cycle A

Then he went and washed and came back able to see. John 9:7

Read *John 9:1–7* as well as *Matthew 8:5–13, Luke 5:12–13,* and *James 5:14–15.* What qualities or attitudes are connected with healing in these Scripture passages?

_____

_____

_____

Our **Global** Community

Hospice Care

The word *hospice* comes from the Latin word *hospitium* meaning "guest house." During the 1960s, the term took on new meaning as British doctors began to specialize in pain-management care specifically for dying patients. The first hospice program in the United States was established in New Haven, Connecticut, in 1974. Today there are more than three thousand hospice programs in the United States, including Puerto Rico and Guam. Most hospice programs include in-home or institutional care and family grief counseling.

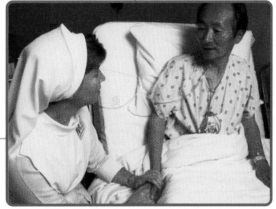

Healing Action

Scripture tells us that sick people were brought to Jesus and that he laid his healing hands on them. (See *Mark 6:5.*) One story centers on a Roman centurion who sought help from Jesus for his paralyzed servant. (See *Matthew 8:5–13.*) Though the soldier and Jesus were socially and culturally very different, Jesus saw past their differences and healed the centurion's servant. Instead of ignoring the soldier because of his political and social beliefs, Jesus used the occasion to show his generosity and compassion—not just for those who suffer, but for those who care for the suffering.

We are called to have the same compassion when we celebrate the Sacrament of the Anointing of the Sick. The sacrament can be celebrated in many different ways. It can be celebrated for an individual or with a group of people who are ill. We can celebrate it in church, at home, or at a hospital. We can celebrate the sacrament in any of three ways: as part of Mass, together with the Sacraments of Reconciliation and Eucharist, or by itself. And because we sometimes face serious illness more than once, the Sacrament of the Anointing of the Sick can be celebrated as

often as it is needed. In any situation, though, the rite includes the Liturgy of the Word and the *Liturgy of Anointing,* during which the anointing takes place.

As part of the Liturgy of Anointing, those gathered join in a litany for those who are sick. Following this litany, there is a *laying on of hands.* Just as Jesus laid hands on the suffering, so the priest lays his hands on one who is ill. Through this action, the Holy Spirit gives strength. Next, the priest prays over the oil and anoints at least the forehead and hands of the person who is sick. Finally, everyone prays a concluding prayer, usually followed by the Lord's Prayer.

In the Sacrament of the Anointing of the Sick, we pray for physical and spiritual healing. God gives strength, peace, and courage—gifts that offer comfort. Through this sacrament, those who suffer are united more closely with Christ and his suffering. For some, suffering may take on new meaning and help them be a part of Jesus' saving work in the world through his Church. They are witnesses for others through their faithfulness. Anointing of the Sick also joins those who are ill more closely with the Church. They are supported by the prayers of the whole Church and can offer their suffering for the good of the Body of Christ.

A Sacrament for Strength Before the Second Vatican Council (1962–1965), the Sacrament of the Anointing of the Sick was called *Extreme Unction,* which means "last anointing." The sacrament was referred to in this way because it was viewed as a ritual for the dying. It came to be associated with the Sacrament of Reconciliation received when dying. Moreover, in the Middle Ages, when the term *Extreme Unction* originated, most people did not live as long as they do today—many did not reach the age of forty-five. Medical treatment was not good. People became ill and died from diseases that are easily prevented or cured today. People expected sickness to lead to death rather than to healing and recovery. For that reason, they wanted to do everything they could to help the person who was ill prepare for death. However, since the Second Vatican Council, the sacrament has come to be understood as more than a preparation for death. It is also about healing and seeking strength from the Holy Spirit for those whose health is made fragile by serious illness or old age.

For further information: Talk with your family and your pastor about their personal experiences with the Sacrament of the Anointing of the Sick. You may also wish to speak with a librarian to find resources that can help you trace the practice of Extreme Unction through history.

Facing **Death**

Although the Sacrament of the Anointing of the Sick may be celebrated by those who are not near death, we sometimes celebrate the sacrament as part of what is called **last rites.** These rites include Reconciliation, Anointing of the Sick, and Eucharist and are meant to prepare a person as he or she ends the earthly life and begins the eternal one. In fact, the Eucharist given to a dying person is called **viaticum,** which means "bread for the journey." These sacraments are the means by which Christ offers spiritual healing to a dying person. Those who celebrate these sacraments often experience great peace as they approach death.

Catholics also have prayers and rites for those who are dying or who have died. Together with the Church community, we express our hope that the dead are now with God eternally. We are sad and we mourn, but our grief is lessened by our faith in Christ, who saved us from everlasting death.

As part of our celebration of the life of a person who has died, we join together for a wake, or a prayerful gathering of friends and family, and a **funeral.** A funeral includes the rites and ceremonies associated with saying good-bye to the person who has died. For Catholics, a funeral Mass and prayers at the grave site are said.

The Healing **Church**

Because we belong to the Body of Christ, the Church, we are called to be healers. Through social services, care centers, hospitals, clinics, and other organizations, Catholics offer medical and spiritual support to those who are sick or dying throughout the world. These services are all part of the Church's mission.

You, too, can help in healing others. You can visit those who are suffering and pray with and for them. You can be useful in ways that may seem insignificant but that could be critically important to the person who needs help, such as getting groceries or medicine, cleaning the house, writing letters, and especially just talking with the person.

Through the Sacrament of the Anointing of the Sick, the Spirit strengthens those who suffer spiritually and physically. And through our experience of the sacrament and of those who are suffering, we can learn how to draw strength in times of pain and loss.

Share with your Faith Partner your experiences of healing.

Catholics Believe

The Anointing of the Sick is not only for those who are dying but for those who are suffering from serious illness or old age.
See Catechism, #1514.

How can we be of assistance to those who are sick, elderly, or dying?

_____

_____

_____

Healing and **Hope**

When we face serious illness or physical suffering, we celebrate the Sacrament of the Anointing of the Sick and experience God's healing grace in our lives. We receive the gifts of strength, peace, and courage to face illness and suffering bravely and patiently. We are reminded of God's presence in our lives and know that we have the prayerful support of the Body of Christ, the Church.

Those who are ill may not be physically healed through the Sacrament of the Anointing of the Sick, although this is possible. But both the person who is ill and those with the person should recognize that God is revealed to us when we are ill as well as when we are healthy. God never abandons or forgets us. He always offers us aid, comfort, and strength.

Celebrating this sacrament helps us reflect on the meaning of our lives. It invites us to have faith when we are struggling physically and are at our weakest point. It brings us to a deeper appreciation of our bodies, which are gifts from God.

Reflect on how anointing can heal us both physically and spiritually. Share your thoughts with your Faith Partner.

WRAP UP

- The Sacrament of the Anointing of the Sick is a Sacrament of Healing.

- In the Sacrament of the Anointing of the Sick, the Holy Spirit strengthens us, heals us in spirit, and can heal us physically.

- Just as Jesus healed people in body and spirit, the Church continues Jesus' work of healing.

- The Sacrament of the Anointing of the Sick is celebrated by those who are seriously ill, fragile from old age or long illness, or facing death.

- The strength and peace of the Holy Spirit give comfort and reveal the presence of God with the person who is suffering.

What questions do you have about this chapter?

_____

_____

_____

Heavenly Father,

Remember those who suffer in illness.

If they are in pain, give them comfort.

If they are irritated, give them peace.

If they are depressed, give them hope.

If they are lonely, remind them of your love.

We ask this through Christ our Lord.

Amen.

Around the Group

Discuss the following question as a group.

What is meant by emotional healing?

After everyone has had a chance to share his or her responses, come up with a group answer upon which everyone can agree.

_____

_____

_____

_____

What personal observations do you have about the group discussion and answer?

_____

_____

_____

_____

Briefly . . .

At the beginning of this chapter, you were asked to explore your attitudes and experience of illness and death. With that reflection in mind, think of someone in need of spiritual or physical healing. Write a prayer for that person in the space below.

_____

_____

_____

Honoring the Body

Expressions of Faith—

We show God how much we love him through our thoughts, words, and actions, but we also show God how much we love him by the way we respect our bodies and those of others. We can live in Christ best by keeping healthy, getting plenty of exercise, and eating the right kinds of foods. Being members of Christ's Body means taking care of the bodies that God has given us.

Scripture

I appeal to you therefore, brothers and sisters, by the mercies of God, to present your bodies as a living sacrifice, holy and acceptable to God, which is your spiritual worship. Do not be conformed to this world, but be transformed by the renewing of your minds, so that you may discern what is the will of God—what is good and acceptable and perfect.

Romans 12:1–2   22nd Sunday of Ordinary Time, Cycle A

Think About It—

We hear a lot about the importance of being healthy. We know that it means eating a balanced diet and exercising regularly. Honoring our bodies as gifts from God means more than this, though. It includes appreciating the bodies that God has given us and living so that not only our hearts and minds but also our bodies reflect God's love. Just as we seek goodness with our words, thoughts, and actions, we also need to seek goodness in the way we live physically. Rate on a scale of 1 to 10 (1 being the lowest, 10 the highest) how important you think each of the following should be in your daily routine.

_____ Getting a good night's sleep

_____ Watching television

_____ Surfing the Internet

_____ Eating healthful foods

_____ Spending time with your friends

_____ Shopping

_____ Doing homework

_____ Spending time with your family

_____ Praying

_____ Exercising several times a week

_____ Reading

Skill Steps–

The skill of Honoring the Body consists of actively showing respect for your body and everyone else's. Memorize the following to help you practice honoring the body.

Rest your body so that you won't get run down.

Exercise regularly to keep your body healthy.

Sexuality is sacred and each person's body should be treated as holy.

Practice good hygiene and stay safe.

Eat properly for health and energy.

Clothe yourself modestly.

Talk about the body with respect, and don't make fun of or use vulgar language when talking about anyone's body.

Check It Out–

Place a check mark next to the sentences that apply to you.

○ I appreciate that my body is a gift from God to be treated with respect.

○ I honor not only my own body but also the bodies of others through respectful language and actions.

○ I try to eat properly and dress appropriately.

○ I limit my time watching television and playing video games.

○ I get eight to nine hours of sleep every night.

○ I avoid dangerous activities in which I might hurt myself.

Based on your response, how could you better honor your body?

_____

_____

Closing Prayer–

Father, in your wisdom you gave us physical, mortal bodies. Help us honor our bodies, whether we are healthy or sick, remembering that they are gifts from you and should be treated with respect. May we live our lives worthy to be considered temples of your spirit. Amen.

CHAPTER 8

Matrimony

Heavenly Father, by your plan a man and a woman unite their lives in love. Bless husbands and wives so that they may be patient and forgiving, respectful and loving toward each other all the days of their lives.

Unity

Love

Marriage

What qualities do you think are the most important in a good marriage? Number the qualities listed below on a scale of 1 to 10, with 1 being the most important and 10 the least important.

_____ physical appearance   _____ sense of humor

_____ intelligence   _____ wealth

_____ respect   _____ patience

_____ love   _____ generosity

_____ religion   _____ compassion

What I hope for most if I get married is

_____

_____

Love and Marriage

Books, movies, television shows, and magazines suggest many ways to find and attract the right person—a "soul mate." However, the focus is frequently more on the search for someone to love and be loved by, and less on how to live happily and meaningfully with that person through many years of marriage.

In general, we base our perception of marriage on the relationships of married family members, friends, or neighbors. The lives of people we know can not only offer a realistic view of the positive values of marriage, such as mutual love and respect, but may also show us difficulties that we can learn to resolve or avoid.

In the Sacrament of Matrimony, a husband and wife become one. They are called to love and serve each other as well as their children and extended family. The partners live Christian lives and grow closer to God by sharing their love with others. This is why the Sacrament of Matrimony is called a Sacrament of Service.

Life and Love

God gives us a great gift when we meet someone with whom we want to share our lives. And when a man and a woman decide to spend their lives together, they are gifts to each other. They agree to live together, united in heart and mind, body and spirit. By celebrating the Sacrament of Matrimony, a man and a woman express their desire to share all that they are with each other.

The relationship at the center of a marriage brings great love and joy. God intends marriage for the love and happiness of husband and wife and for their joy in the birth of any children they may have.

The Sacrament of Matrimony is a celebration of this love-giving and life-giving relationship. It creates and maintains a bond between a man and a woman as well as between the couple and God. The faithful love that the couple shares is a reflection of God's love for all of us. Through the Sacrament of Matrimony, Christ strengthens the couple with grace to live and, if they have children, to raise them within the bonds of faith and love.

Celebrating Matrimony

Catholics often celebrate the Sacrament of Matrimony within Mass, but there are occasions when the rite is celebrated outside of Mass. Both celebrations invite God's love and grace into the relationship.

The Rite of Marriage follows the Liturgy of the Word. The presider asks about the couple's freedom to marry each other, their intention to be faithful, and their willingness to accept and raise children.

Catholics Believe

The love between a husband and a wife reminds us of the eternal love with which God loves all humans. See Catechism, #1604.

List several ways that a couple can show their love for God and for each other.

_____

_____

_____

At the heart of the sacrament is the exchange of vows, also called *consent,* or agreement. As they give their complete and free consent to each other before other members of the Body of Christ, the man and woman make a **covenant** before God and his Church. They enter into a sacred and binding promise that establishes their union before God and seeks his grace to keep their vows. The marriage covenant is a sign of the sacred covenant that Christ has with his Church. Through the couple's celebration of the sacrament, God acts in their lives to create a union that is *indissoluble,* a union that cannot be broken.

If it is the custom, the priest blesses the rings and each partner places a ring on the other's finger. The Rite of Marriage ends with the *General Intercessions,* and, at Mass, the Liturgy of the Eucharist follows. The celebration of the Sacrament of Matrimony takes place in a moment of time, but the sacrament is actually lived out over a lifetime.

Living
Marriage
Vows

A **vocation** is the call to live God's love through single life, marriage, religious life, or priesthood. We know what our vocation is by looking into our hearts, opening ourselves to the guidance of the Holy Spirit through prayer, and seeking the guidance of others. We must take into account our talents and abilities and our willingness to respond to what we believe God asks of us. If we are called to the vocation of marriage, we recognize the signs of love and commitment.

OUR CHRISTIAN JOURNEY

A Holy Couple One of the Church's most popular saints is Thérèse of Lisieux (1873–1897), a holy Carmelite nun also known as the Little Flower. In 1997 she became the third woman to be named a Doctor of the Church. What is not as widely known, however, is that her parents were also very religious. Both her father, Louis Martin, and her mother, Azélie-Marie Guérin, had considered a religious vocation when they were young. Eventually, though, each decided to serve God by raising a family and working in a trade—Louis as a watchmaker and Azélie-Marie as a lacemaker. The couple had nine children. Throughout their lives, Louis and Azélie-Marie stressed the importance of a loving, faithful home. As a result, many of their children, including Thérèse, were inspired to enter religious life and to live in service to their Church family and to God.

For further information: Read a biography of Thérèse. You may also wish to research the family's history on the Internet.

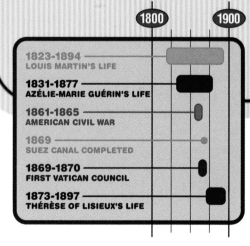

1800   1900

1823–1894
LOUIS MARTIN'S LIFE

1831–1877
AZÉLIE-MARIE GUÉRIN'S LIFE

1861–1865
AMERICAN CIVIL WAR

1869
SUEZ CANAL COMPLETED

1869–1870
FIRST VATICAN COUNCIL

1873–1897
THÉRÈSE OF LISIEUX'S LIFE

We accept the responsibilities that will come with this way of life, and we accept the person whom we love for all that he or she is—which means accepting both weaknesses and strengths.

One of the most important responsibilities in marriage is *faithfulness*. This means that a husband and wife commit themselves exclusively to each other, both in love and sexual fidelity. A husband and wife are to be faithful to each other as Christ is faithful to his Church.

Of course, there are challenges in every marriage. These may include communication, financial issues, disciplining children, illnesses, and disabilities. God does not abandon a couple when they need him, nor does the Church, which provides marriage counseling and volunteer services to help families with such things as financial counseling and disability assistance. Each day the couple needs to recommit themselves to each other and respond to the grace of the Sacrament of Matrimony.

Not every married person succeeds in living this sacrament for life. If a couple is married in the Catholic Church, their union, because it is a sacrament, cannot be broken except under special circumstances. A couple may choose to obtain a civil divorce to protect their legal rights. But only when the Church determines that the marriage was not valid from the beginning will the Church issue a declaration of nullity, or an *annulment*. Reasons for a declaration of nullity are extremely serious, such as the lack of free consent by either partner at the time of the marriage. Unless a marriage has been annulled, the couple cannot remarry in the Church.

Focus On

Marriage Vows

Marriage vows are not merely promises a man and a woman make to each other; they are promises a man and a woman make to God. In the Catholic Church, marriage is a public celebration; that is, it must take place before two witnesses and a properly authorized minister. Like the other Western Churches, the Latin Rite of the Catholic Church teaches that the partners confer the sacrament upon each other; the Eastern Rites and the Orthodox Churches, however, teach that the presiding priest confers the sacrament on the couple.

Family Life

Because God created us to love and to cooperate with his plan to give life, marriage is intended to be both love-giving and life-giving. This means that, in addition to their commitment to love each other, the couple should be open to the possibility of having children.

Whether they have children or not, though, all married couples live as members of a family, often referred to as the **domestic Church.** The family is the core of the Church because our faith begins in the home and is continually nourished by our families. As members of a family, we are taught to pray, love, forgive, support, and guide each other in faith. The family as *domestic Church* points to the important role families of all kinds play in the life of the Church.

As part of the sacrament, a husband and wife agree to grow as a family. In return, the love that unites them can become a source of great joy, wisdom, and courage. The lives they lead can truly be lived in service to others because they can share themselves with others.

A happy marriage and family life give us a glimpse of what the kingdom of God is like. The kingdom of God has been described as a banquet and as a wedding feast. (See *Matthew 25:1–10*.)

For us the covenant that is created during the celebration of Matrimony is a celebration for the entire Church. The Body of Christ rejoices at the bond of love that two people share because it is strengthened when a man and a woman vow to share their lives in love.

Opening the Word

2nd Sunday of Ordinary Time, Cycle C

On the third day there was a wedding in Cana of Galilee, and the mother of Jesus was there. Jesus and his disciples had also been invited to the wedding. John 2:1–2

Read *John 2:1–12* as well as *Proverbs 31:10–12, 1 Corinthians 13:4–7,* and *Ephesians 5:28–33.* What messages about marriage found in these readings apply to marriage today?

_____

_____

_____

_____

_____

_____

_____

Share your responses and thoughts with your Faith Partner.

FAITH PARTNERSHIP

In the Home

One of the most important aspects of the Sacrament of Matrimony is its focus on the family. The people with whom we share our lives form our first community of faith, our domestic Church. There are times when, for one reason or another, some families don't live as the domestic Church, but most of the time our families are the first place we learn to live our faith. As we grow older and become more independent, our families will play different roles in our lives. Yet it is natural that the people to whom we are closest and with whom we share the most are also the ones who encourage our faith and help us grow closer to God. Our domestic Church is found wherever these special people are.

Each day, with every choice and action, we shape who we will become as adults. For now, we are living out the vocation of single life. As such, we develop the virtues and skills that are a part of that vocation. We choose to live honestly, chastely, and faithfully. We create healthy friendships, we share time with our families, and we use our talents to help others. If, as adults, we choose religious life or marriage, we will make many of the same commitments to a religious community or to a spouse. Some will be different, but they will all revolve around the lessons we learned as members of our families.

Reflect on how a family at its best is to be a domestic Church. Share your thoughts with your Faith Partner.

FaiTH ParTNeRSHiP

WRAP UP

- •The Sacrament of Matrimony is one of the Sacraments of Service.
- •The Sacrament of Matrimony celebrates the bond of love between a man and a woman.
- •Marriage is both love-giving and life-giving.
- •Marriage reminds us of the faithfulness and unity that exist between Christ and his Church.
- •The family is meant to be the domestic Church.

What questions do you have about this chapter?

_____

_____

_____

Around the Group

Discuss the following question as a group.

How would you explain the following saying? "You don't marry a person, you marry into a family."

After everyone has had a chance to share his or her responses, come up with a group answer upon which everyone can agree.

_____

_____

_____

_____

What personal observations do you have about the group discussion and answer?

_____

_____

_____

_____

Briefly...

At the beginning of this chapter, you were asked to prioritize certain characteristics in a potential marriage partner. Reflecting on these qualities, write a recipe for a good friendship or marriage.

_____   _____

_____   _____

_____   _____

_____   _____

_____

_____

_____

_____

Honoring the Body

Expressions of Faith-

Just as a loving and committed husband and wife treat each other with respect, so too must we practice the skill of Honoring the Body in our single lives. We must choose attitudes and actions that demonstrate our commitment to the way Jesus wants us to live. We understand that while our interest and affection for others is normal and healthy, we must avoid treating anyone's body selfishly or thoughtlessly. We recognize that our gift of sexuality comes with the responsibility of treating each other with kindness and respect.

Scripture

. . . do you not know that your body is a temple of the Holy Spirit within you, which you have from God, and that you are not your own?

1 Corinthians 6:19   2nd Sunday of Ordinary Time, Cycle B

Skill Steps-

The skill of Honoring the Body requires us to RESPECT our bodies. We need to remember to get rest, exercise, use our sexuality as the special gift that it is, practice good hygiene and stay safe, eat properly, clothe ourselves appropriately, talk about our own bodies and the bodies of others with respect, and avoid vulgar language.

Here are some things to remember:

- Our bodies are gifts from God to be appreciated and treated with respect.
- Being members of Christ's Body means taking care of the bodies that God has given us.
- Not only our hearts and minds but also our bodies reflect God's love.
- We show respect for others by honoring their bodies, keeping them from harm or injury.

Skill Builder-

Do you think that our society and the media support the Christian practice of honoring the body? On the lines below, write down the titles of a movie, a song, and a TV program that you like. Next, rate how each of your choices honors or dishonors the body by giving it a grade of A, B, C, D, or F. When deciding the grade, consider how the body is shown and what kinds of habits or behaviors are shown or described.

Share your thoughts with your Faith Partner.

	Title	Grade
Movie	_____	_____
Song	_____	_____
TV program	_____	_____

Putting It into Practice-

For each letter of the word RESPECT and its meaning, suggest one concrete way someone your age could honor his or her body. For example, for the letter *R*, tell how much rest you think someone your age needs each day, including the hours of sleep you think are necessary. Mention any other ideas you have for resting or relaxing, such as quiet hobbies.

Closing Prayer-

Loving Father, you have created us to support and love one another as members of our families. Guide us as we decide on a vocation, and teach us how to best live in your service. Be with us as we live our lives, and help us treat ourselves and others with respect.

Holy Orders

Almighty God, remember your Church. Give our pope and bishops wisdom and courage. Help our priests and deacons serve you in the name of your Son, Jesus Christ. Amen.

Who are some of the people to whom you look for advice, guidance, and support? Identify them by name or by initials.

_____

_____

_____

_____

How do you decide whether or not to ask someone for advice or support? What kind of person does he or she have to be?

_____

_____

_____

_____

Mission to Serve

Each of us looks to the people we trust for advice. Our friends, teachers, family members, and coaches help guide us when we have difficulty making a decision or when we get into trouble.

By celebrating the Sacrament of Holy Orders, a Sacrament of Service, the deacons, priests, and bishops of the Church serve God by serving God's people. They are consecrated and given a special power by Christ, for the benefit of his Church, to preside at the sacraments and preach the gospel.

Our Priesthood in **Christ**

You probably don't realize all the little ways you serve others every day. Think about the times when you have befriended someone in your class who was being picked on or ignored, or when you listened sympathetically to a friend who was worrying about a problem in his or her life. Or perhaps you did a small good deed for someone without being asked. These were times when you served others.

Opening the Word

And he appointed twelve, whom he also named apostles, to be with him, and to be sent out to proclaim the message. Mark 3:14

Read *Mark 3:13–19* as well as *Acts 6:1–6, Hebrews 5:1–10,* and *1 Timothy 3:1–7.* According to Scripture, what are some tasks of leaders of the Church?

_____

_____

_____

Jesus asked all his followers to serve others every day because through living the message of the gospel, we can come to know God's love for us. As we begin to understand and experience his love, we will, with God's grace, share it with others through the gifts of our time, talents, patience, and support.

In the Sacrament of Baptism, we are united with Christ. We are made part of his Body and are promised eternal life with him in his Father's kingdom. Through Baptism we become members of the priesthood of all believers, also called the **common priesthood.** We live our common priesthood when we show people what it means to be a Christian by the way we live. When we teach others, care for them, and encourage their faith, we live as members of the priesthood of all believers.

Religious Vows

Religious vows are special promises made to God, usually by those who have chosen to become members of a religious community. These vows most often include poverty, chastity, and obedience, and may be temporary or permanent.

In Service

The Ordained Priesthood

In addition to the common priesthood, deacons, priests, and bishops are part of what is called the **ministerial priesthood.** The word *ministerial* means to serve God by serving others. Through the sacrament of Holy Orders, men are ordained as priests and bishops to celebrate sacraments, especially the Eucharist. Though deacons cannot preside at Mass, they can celebrate Baptism and Matrimony and preside at funeral rites outside of Mass. Bishops, priests, and deacons preach and teach the word of God and serve, support, and guide the Body of Christ.

When a man is ordained, he receives the grace to serve the Church in the name of Jesus. As part of the ordination, the candidate receives a *sacramental character* to mark the fact that he has become Christ's in a special way. Most priests in the Latin Rite or Western Church promise to live a life of *celibacy,* which means that they do not marry. As celibates, they can give their lives to the service of the Body of Christ.

There are three degrees of priesthood: deacons, priests, and bishops. As such, the Church celebrates three different ordination ceremonies. Each ceremony focuses on the specific calling of those being ordained. Each ceremony includes the laying on of hands and a prayer of consecration.

The ordination of a deacon celebrates the candidate's service to the local parish and to the bishop and priests. During the ceremony the deacon is asked to make a commitment to serve his bishop and to minister to the people. At the end of the ordination, the deacon is presented with his vestments, the stole and the dalmatic, a robe-like vestment.

Some men are ordained transitional deacons while they are preparing for the priesthood. Other men don't wish to become priests and, instead, become permanent deacons. A deacon wears his stole, a narrow band of cloth, over his left shoulder.

Deacons serve the common priesthood by baptizing, witnessing and blessing marriages, and by preaching and teaching the word of God, among other activities. A deacon cannot preside at the Eucharist, Reconciliation, or the Anointing of the Sick.

The deacon is also ordained to do works of charity. He may visit parishioners who are sick, prepare couples for marriage, and help with the parish youth program. Does your parish have a deacon? If so, in what ministries is he involved?

A Good Listener Saint John Vianney was noted for his saintliness and for his remarkable ability as a confessor. Ironically, this saint very nearly failed to become a priest. He began studying for the priesthood when he was eighteen, but he could not do the work required and was dismissed from the seminary in 1814. A local priest intervened, tutoring John and arranging for him to be tested and interviewed by seminary officials. John returned to the seminary and was finally ordained, and in 1818 he became the parish priest of a little village called Ars. Through the care and attention he gave to his community, he was able to strengthen and guide the people to a better understanding of their faith. Except for brief interruptions, he spent more than twelve hours a day in the confessional, bringing God's grace and reconciliation to troubled spirits. John Vianney is the patron saint of priests, and his feast day is August 9.

For further information: Research the life of Saint John Vianney in a book about the history of saints. You may also wish to find out whether your diocese includes any churches named after him.

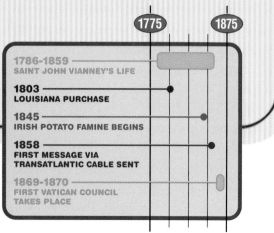

1775   **1875**

1786–1859
SAINT JOHN VIANNEY'S LIFE

1803
LOUISIANA PURCHASE

1845
IRISH POTATO FAMINE BEGINS

1858
FIRST MESSAGE VIA
TRANSATLANTIC CABLE SENT

1869–1870
FIRST VATICAN COUNCIL
TAKES PLACE

To Represent Christ

When a priest is ordained, he represents Christ as priest, prophet, and king. During the ceremony the celebrating bishop presents the priest with his vestments, the stole and chasuble (a cape-like garment), and anoints the hands of the new priest. The bishop then presents him with the chalice and paten, inviting him to imitate the mystery of Jesus' saving actions by the way he lives his life. Through a promise of obedience, and the kiss of peace from the bishop at the end of the ordination liturgy, the priest is made a coworker with the bishops of the Church.

Today, most priests work in parishes, and we most often experience a priest's ministry during Mass. Priests are ordained to preach the gospel, lead the faith community, and preside at the sacraments, especially Eucharist and Reconciliation. The priest also serves as a counselor, administrator, and a religious guide to answer questions we have about our faith.

Discuss with your Faith Partner the things about the priesthood that interest you.

FaiTH PaRTNeRSHiP

By means of the ministerial priesthood, Christ builds up and leads the Church. *See Catechism, #1547.*

Describe the ideal bishop, priest, or deacon.

_____

_____

_____

Shepherds of the Church

As sanctifiers, teachers, and rulers, bishops share in the priesthood of Jesus in a special way. The ordination of a bishop is the fullness of the Sacrament of Holy Orders. Through the celebration of the sacrament, bishops receive the mission that was first given to the apostles—to preach the gospel. During the ceremony the bishop-elect, as he is called, is anointed on the forehead and is presented with the symbols of his office: the Book of Gospels to show that he is to proclaim the word of God;

a ring to show his faithfulness to the Church; the *crosier,* or staff, to show he is our shepherd; and the *miter,* a pointed cap of stiffened cloth, a reminder that followers of Christ are clothed with holiness.

Bishops are called the shepherds of the Church because they, like the apostles before them, have been directed by Christ to watch over his Church. Unlike most deacons and priests, bishops care for a diocese. And together with the other bishops and the pope, they lead the entire Church community.

Because a bishop has many responsibilities and a large territory, we do not often see him. But your bishop's actions affect you in many ways that you probably don't realize. Some of the decisions a bishop makes, together with his administrative staff, include those in areas of religious education, youth ministry, and charitable projects.

Together, deacons, priests, and bishops share in the mission of Christ. They serve, teach, and guide us as members of the Body of Christ. By devoting their lives to God and the Church in this special way, they live out their vocations and enable us to grow closer to God.

In Service to All

As members of the common priesthood, we work with those in the ministerial priesthood to spread the good news and to serve others. We might give encouragement to a younger brother or sister, or visit an elderly or sick parish member with a parent or grandparent. With the help of teachers and classmates, we might even start a discussion about racism or violence in schools.

When we generously offer our talents and abilities to the Body of Christ, we work with the ministerial priesthood to strengthen the Church. As head of his Body, Christ continues his work in the world through all of us who belong to him. In any vocation to which God calls us—single life, married, or ordained—we can grow in our relationship with God and with one another.

Have you thought about the vocation to which you might be called? Remember to seek the wisdom and counsel of the Spirit as you prepare for the time when you will decide what is right for you, and how you may best serve God and his Church.

Reflect on three specific things you can do to exercise your common priesthood. Share your thoughts with your Faith Partner.

WRAP UP

- Holy Orders is one of the Sacraments of Service.
- The Body of Christ is a community of the priesthood of all believers, also called the common priesthood.
- There are three degrees of ministerial priesthood: deacons, priests, and bishops.
- To be ordained means to be consecrated, set apart by Christ for his Church.

What questions do you have about this chapter?

_____

_____

_____

Around the Group

Discuss the following question as a group.

What are the two most important qualities needed as a deacon, priest, or bishop?

After everyone has had a chance to share his or her responses, come up with a group answer upon which everyone can agree.

_____

_____

_____

_____

What personal observations do you have about the group discussion and answer?

_____

_____

_____

_____

Briefly . . .

At the beginning of this chapter, you were asked to consider the kind of person you would approach for advice and support. What qualities do you share with this person, and in what ways do these qualities help you share the common priesthood with a deacon or priest in your parish or community?

_____

_____

_____

Keeping Promises

Expressions of Faith

Keeping promises is an important part of living as a follower of Christ, whether we are married, single, or ordained. The ability to keep promises shows that we are people of strong character. It shows that we are trustworthy and responsible.

Scripture

"Let your word be 'Yes, Yes' or 'No, No'; anything more than this comes from the evil one."
Matthew 5:37   6th Sunday of Ordinary Time, Cycle A

Think About It

All of us make promises. We promise our friends that we will keep their secrets. We promise our families that we will be responsible. Some promises are easy to keep. Others shouldn't be made in the first place. And still others challenge us to work tirelessly, calling on the very best that is in us.

A young college basketball player left school after his sophomore year to turn pro. While playing for the NBA, he took correspondence courses during the season and attended classes during the off-season. Just three years later he got his degree. He went to his graduation ceremony in the afternoon and flew back in time to play for his team the same evening. That night the team organization allowed any fan who came to the game with a college ID to get in for only $10. When reporters asked the new graduate about his achievement, he replied that he had promised his mother that he would finish his degree. On this exciting day, he and his family celebrated the fulfillment of that promise.

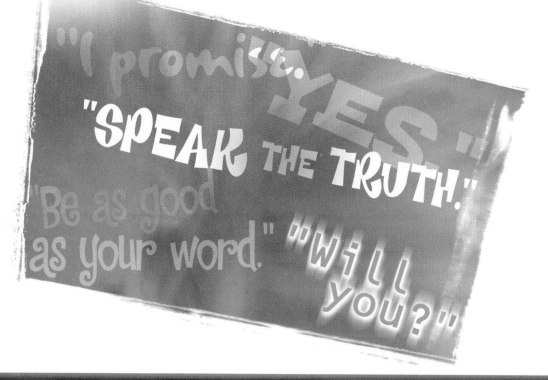

Skill Steps-

Every promise you make will show what kind of person you really are.
Here are some *Dos* and *Don'ts* of keeping promises.

Do

Consider the motive behind the promise (both your own and that of the person asking for the promise)—*before you make it.* Is the motive a good one?

Consider the cost involved with the promise—*before you make it.* Can you do what it takes?

Say "I made a promise." When keeping a promise conflicts with someone or something else, simply come right out and say that you are under the obligation of a promise. People will understand and respect you for staying faithful to the promise you made.

Sacrifice. You may have to give up other things in order to keep your integrity, keep your word, and fulfill your promise.

Don't

Make promises automatically or quickly. Most of the time it's not necessary to promise—your "yes" or "no" should be good enough.

Make promises lightly. Every promise brings responsibility. Every promise will show the kind of person you are.

Keep a promise if someone is being hurt or endangered by it.

Keep a promise that makes you feel uncomfortable or worried. Tell a trusted adult.

Do something immoral in order to keep a promise (lying, being cruel, and so on).

Check It Out-

Place a check mark next to those statements with which you agree.

○ People count on me because my word is good.

○ I like it when people trust me because they know the truth is important to me.

○ I follow Jesus' example of being willing to make sacrifices to keep my promises.

How good is your word? Circle one of the responses below.

People can count on me.   It depends.

Not so good.   Don't believe a word I say.

What goal can you set for yourself to become better at keeping promises?

_____

Closing Prayer-

We place ourselves before you, Lord our God, with thanks for all you have given us. Guide the leaders of your Church. And give us the strength and courage to fulfill our promises. Amen.

Continuing
Our **Promise**

Heavenly Father,
challenge us
to share the
message of your
love. Dare us to
live honestly.
Urge us to
stand up for
our beliefs and
to speak out
against injustice.
Confront us
with the truth
about ourselves.

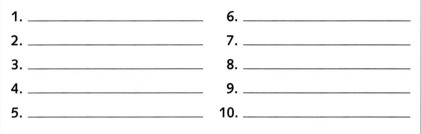

What Do You Think?

On the lines below, create a Top Ten list of what you think makes your life worthwhile.

1. _____
2. _____
3. _____
4. _____
5. _____

6. _____
7. _____
8. _____
9. _____
10. _____

What will your life be like in ten years? Describe what you think you will be doing and what you think you will be like.

_____

_____

_____

_____

The Good Life?

Adolescence is a busy and sometimes confusing time. Friendships change. Family relationships change. The decisions we make are more difficult than those we made just a few years ago.

As an adolescent, you may feel pressured to try drugs or sex in order to be part of a group. Perhaps things have been so bad at times that you have even considered suicide. No matter what, you always have the need to feel accepted and loved. How can the sacraments and your faith help you deal with these issues?

For Christians the good life is the life that Christ offers us. It is the virtuous life that helps us grow in faith and love. Through the sacraments God offers us the spiritual nourishment and strength to make good decisions and to live in healthy relationships with others.

Living the
Sacraments

Participating in the sacraments is important in developing a faith life. Through the sacraments we experience God's saving love in rituals that celebrate life, nourishment, reconciliation, healing, and service. We become aware of our relationship with God—the Father, Son, and Spirit.

But in order to fully appreciate the sacraments, we need to see past the actual rite to recognize how Christ can transform our lives. For example, our celebration of the Sacraments of Christian Initiation doesn't end after we celebrate the rites of Baptism, Eucharist, or Confirmation. Because we become members of Christ's Body, we are called to change the way we think and act. As members of the Church community, we should live as signs of God at work in the world—we should live as sacraments.

Catholics Believe

Prayer is a surge of the heart, embracing both sadness and joy.
See Catechism, #2558.

Sketch a picture or write a poem that expresses your feelings about prayer.

Share your thoughts with your Faith Partner.

Focus On

The Lord's Prayer

The Lord's Prayer we pray during Mass is based on two Gospel passages, *Matthew 6:9–13* and *Luke 11:2–4.* Many people have recognized the importance of this prayer to their individual lives and to the life of the Church. For example, Saint Thomas Aquinas called it the most perfect private prayer.

Through the Sacraments of Initiation we are brought into a community that witnesses to the work of Christ. Through Baptism and Confirmation we are joined to a group of people who care about us. This group wants only what is best for us. Members of the Body of Christ can help us make good decisions that will affect our lives in a positive way.

As part of the Church family, we gather together to be nourished through the Sacrament of the Eucharist. In this sacrament we receive God's love and strength to help us deal with the problems and temptations we face. In fact, each of us can become a sacrament to others by being a sign of love and strength to them. We can look for opportunities to listen to and care for others in a respectful and loving way.

In Reconciliation, one of the Sacraments of Healing, we are forgiven for those times when we have sinned. We, in turn, are better able to forgive others when they hurt us or damage our relationship. We can be peacemakers by trying to resolve arguments or conflicts between friends or family members.

People around us may be suffering because they do not feel accepted and loved. Some may be experiencing physical or emotional abuse. There are many occasions when people need us to reach out to them and be sensitive to what they are feeling. At these times we can bring healing into their lives.

Sometimes a young person can get very sick or be in a serious accident. When this happens, the Sacrament of the Anointing of the Sick—the other Sacrament of Healing—can bring God's grace, love, and forgiveness to him or her. It is especially during these unexpected times that the members of the Body of Christ offer comfort to one another.

The Sacraments of Service are ways in which adults answer God's call to serve others through marriage or ordination. You may eventually make the decision to follow the vocation of marriage or priesthood. Or you may choose religious life or the single life. But for now you should pray for God's guidance and think about what future vocation will allow you to best use your gifts and abilities.

One important way we prepare ourselves for this decision is by developing healthy relationships. Through our friendships and family relationships, we learn about our strengths and weaknesses. We learn to be honest with others and with ourselves. Most of all, we learn respect. We learn to respect people as they are now, and to respect who they can become with God's grace.

As Christians we must care for others and never use people for our own benefit. To do so would go against everything that Jesus taught. He called us to be servants to others. And when we share the gift of ourselves and show others the respect they deserve, we are living lives of service.

A Woman of Caring

Mother Teresa founded the Missionaries of Charity, a religious order of women dedicated to caring for those who are sick and dying among the poorest people in the world. Mother Teresa was born in Macedonia but spent most of her life in India. When she was just eighteen, she joined a group of Irish sisters and was sent to India to teach in a high school for the daughters of wealthy families. In the late 1940s she began her vocation of caring for those who were poor. She taught children who lived in the slums of Calcutta, cared for those who were sick, and eased the suffering of those who were dying. Eventually, a number of young women joined her in her work, and in 1950 she organized the Missionaries of Charity. Since then the sisters of her order have established hospitals and schools throughout the world. In 1979 Mother Teresa received the Nobel Peace Prize for her work. Believed by many to be a saint, Mother Teresa died in 1997.

For further information: Research the Missionaries of Charity on the Internet or read about the life of Mother Teresa in one of her many biographies.

1900		2000

1910–1997
MOTHER TERESA'S LIFE

1914–1918
WORLD WAR I

1948
STATE OF ISRAEL ESTABLISHED

1962–1965
SECOND VATICAN COUNCIL

2000
JUBILEE YEAR

The Prayer in Our Hearts

Like the practice of the sacraments, prayer helps us live as God intended. Through prayer we grow in our faith life and reflect on being sacraments. Prayer is raising our minds and hearts to God. We pray with our thoughts, words, and actions.

When we think of prayer, we usually picture ourselves communicating individually with God. We could be in a church, at the park, or at school. This **personal prayer** is very important to us as we develop our faith. As members of the Body of Christ, we often join together with others in church or elsewhere for **communal prayer.** The most important communal prayer is liturgy.

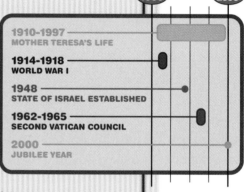

From the heights of joy to the depths of grief, we can turn to God in prayer. Before our meals we ask God's blessing on our food and bless God in return for providing for us. We adore him for the awesome God he is. We humbly ask him for the things we need and for help in facing the many challenges and pressures of our lives. We ask God's forgiveness when we sin and when we choose selfishness at the expense of others. We pray for others who are close to us or who may be far away but whose needs are ours in the Body of Christ. We thank God for the many gifts and joys of our lives. We praise God, who is the source and goal of our lives.

Our Life
in Christ

When we celebrate the sacraments and when we pray, we realize that Christ is present in our lives. He is with us when we find it easy to live virtuous lives, and he is with us when we are struggling to understand how to live as he wants. Christ is with us when our friends believe the worst about us, when our parents don't understand us, and when our teachers and coaches are pushing us to do our best. We can count on him to be there to guide us no matter what we are experiencing.

Throughout our lives, we will experience the breakup of some friendships and the development of new ones. But there is one friend who will never leave us and who will always love us—Jesus. Jesus is our Savior, brother, and friend. Each of us has experienced both good and bad times. Maybe the bad times were caused by a parent who didn't really understand our problem, or by a friend or peer who let us down. Whatever the cause, Jesus is always there to share the good and the bad times. We can talk to him anytime and

anywhere, and he will listen. Because Jesus was once our age, he understands what our needs are. Like us, he was also tempted. He experienced suffering and death. Jesus is the sacrament of all sacraments. With Jesus by our side, we will never be alone or unloved.

Opening the Word

Ascension of the Lord, Cycle A

"... I am with you always, to the end of the age." Matthew 28:20

Read *Matthew 28:16–20* as well as *Romans 12:3–8, Ephesians 2:19–22,* and *Colossians 3:12–17.* What does it mean to be a Christian?

_____

_____

_____

_____

Living Our Faith

Some people say they are Christians, but they mistreat their friends and often deceive their families. Other people don't say very much about what they believe, but they set a good example of faithfulness. How we present ourselves, how we treat those closest to us, and how we behave toward those we barely know tell the world who we really are.

To be united with Christ and to be a member of his Body by virtue of our Baptism should mean something in our daily living. It should mean that Christ directs our actions, informs our ideals, and guides our lives.

No one reaches the height of his or her faith life immediately and becomes close to God all at once. Things that seem insignificant at the moment may be quite important in terms of our faith life and how we develop as people of character. For example, it counts when we overlook an insult. It counts when we share our talents with those who need us. And it counts when we tell the truth at a time when it is hard to do so.

All of us have challenges to face every day. Resisting the temptation to have a beer, turning down cigarettes or drugs, and avoiding sexual activity can be the measure of how well our faith works to help us become people of integrity. That's why the sacraments are so important in our lives. Through them, the Holy Spirit gives us the grace we need to live every day as Christ would.

Reflect on how we can be Christ-like in our relationships. Share your thoughts with your Faith Partner.

FaiTH ParTNeRSHiP

WRAP UP

- •We meet Jesus in the sacraments.
- •We recognize Jesus as our brother and most loyal friend, the one whose friendship with us never falters and never ends.
- •We grow in our faith life through the sacraments and prayer.
- •We are called to live the sacraments.
- •Jesus taught us to pray the Lord's Prayer, which has been called the perfect prayer for the members of his Body.

What questions do you have about this chapter?

_____

_____

_____

Around the Group

Discuss the following question as a group.

What does it mean to be a Catholic?

After everyone has had a chance to share his or her response, come up with a group answer upon which everyone can agree.

_____
_____
_____
_____

What personal observations do you have about the group discussion and answer?

_____
_____
_____
_____

Briefly...

At the beginning of this chapter, you were asked to create a list of things that make your life worthwhile. Ask a family member or friend to make a list of things that he or she thinks make life worthwhile. Compare that list with the one you made. How many items are the same? Why do you think there are differences between the two lists?

Keeping Promises

Expressions of Faith—

Our life in Christ goes back to the promises made at Baptism. These promises rejected sin and set the direction of our lives as being lived for Christ. Every time we celebrate a sacrament, we are keeping the promises made at our Baptism.

Scripture

"But the Advocate, the Holy Spirit, whom the Father will send in my name, will teach you everything, and remind you of all that I have said to you."

John 14:26   6th Sunday of Easter, Cycle C

Skill Steps—

Remember that making and keeping promises is a skill that we use all our lives. We know that we will be judged on how good our word is, and we know that sometimes it isn't easy to keep our word.

Here are some key points to remember:

● Keeping promises is an important part of living as a follower of Jesus.

● The ability to keep a promise shows that we are trustworthy and responsible.

● Promises can require sacrifices.

● Consider whether a promise should be made and what would be involved in keeping it.

Skill Builder—

To some extent, all of our relationships involve promises.

What is one of the promises we make to God or that God makes to us in each of the sacraments?

1. Baptism _____

2. Confirmation _____

3. Eucharist _____

4. Reconciliation _____

5. Anointing of the Sick _____

6. Matrimony _____

7. Holy Orders _____

Share your responses and thoughts with your Faith Partner.

Putting It into Practice–

How well are you making and keeping promises? Have you broken a promise recently? Are you struggling to keep a promise? Are you facing sacrifices that will have to be made? Do you have to re-establish your priorities in order to keep your word?

For each category below, identify a promise that you have made. You can use a word, a symbol, or an initial. Then rate how well you are doing with the promise. Finally, decide what you will have to do next to keep your promise.

Promise Made With	Promise	Rating	What To Do Next
God	_____	_____	_____
Church	_____	_____	_____
Parent	_____	_____	_____
Family Member	_____	_____	_____
Self	_____	_____	_____

Keeping promises is a skill that affects every part of our lives. It affects the relationship we have with our families, how we interact with our friends, and to what extent we live as faithful members of the Body of Christ.

Based on what you have learned about this skill, what do you think are your strengths when it comes to making promises?

_____

_____

What are some things you need to work on?

_____

_____

Closing Prayer–

Lord, we aren't sure what our futures hold, but we know you will be there for us. We know we can count on your love and strength and encouragement. We promise that we will remember to turn to you because in guiding us, you reveal yourself to us. Help us become the people you want us to be. Draw us closer to you. Amen.

Prayers and **Resources**

The Lord's Prayer

Our Father, who art in heaven,
hallowed be thy name;
thy kingdom come;
thy will be done on earth as it is in heaven.
Give us this day our daily bread;
and forgive us our trespasses
as we forgive those who trespass against us;
and lead us not into temptation,
but deliver us from evil.
Amen.

Hail Mary

Hail, Mary, full of grace,
the Lord is with you!
Blessed are you among women,
and blessed is the fruit of your womb, Jesus.
Holy Mary, Mother of God,
pray for us sinners,
now and at the hour of our death.
Amen.

THE TEN COMMANDMENTS

1. I am the Lord your God. You shall not have strange gods before me.

2. You shall not take the name of the Lord your God in vain.

3. Remember to keep holy the Lord's day.

4. Honor your father and your mother.

5. You shall not kill.

6. You shall not commit adultery.

7. You shall not steal.

8. You shall not bear false witness against your neighbor.

9. You shall not covet your neighbor's wife.

10. You shall not covet your neighbor's goods.

THE BEATITUDES

Blessed are the poor in spirit,
   for theirs is the kingdom
   of heaven.

Blessed are they who mourn,
   for they will be comforted.

Blessed are the meek,
   for they will inherit the land.

Blessed are they who hunger and
thirst for righteousness,
   for they will be satisfied.

Blessed are the merciful,
   for they will be shown mercy.

Blessed are the clean of heart,
   for they will see God.

Blessed are the peacemakers,
   for they will be called children
   of God.

Blessed are they who are persecuted
for the sake of righteousness,
   for theirs is the kingdom
   of heaven.

(Matthew 5:3–10)

Glory to the Father (Doxology)

Glory to the Father, and to the Son,
and to the Holy Spirit:
as it was in the beginning, is now,
and will be for ever.
Amen.

Gifts of the Holy Spirit

Wisdom
Understanding
Right judgment (Counsel)
Courage (Fortitude)
Knowledge
Reverence (Piety)
Wonder and awe (Fear of the Lord)

Fruits of the Spirit

Charity
Joy
Peace
Patience
Kindness
Goodness
Generosity
Gentleness
Faithfulness
Modesty
Self-control
Chastity

Act of Contrition

My God,
I am sorry for my sins with all my
heart.
In choosing to do wrong
and failing to do good,
I have sinned against you
whom I should love above all things.
I firmly intend, with your help,
to do penance,
to sin no more,
and to avoid whatever leads me to sin.
Our Savior Jesus Christ
suffered and died for us.
In his name, my God, have mercy.

Works of Mercy

Corporal (for the body)
Feed the hungry.
Give drink to the thirsty.
Clothe the naked.
Shelter the homeless.
Visit the sick.
Visit the imprisoned.
Bury the dead.

Spiritual (for the spirit)
Warn the sinner.
Teach the ignorant.
Counsel the doubtful.
Comfort the sorrowful.
Bear wrongs patiently.
Forgive injuries.
Pray for the living and the dead.

PRECEPTS OF THE CHURCH

1. Take part in the Mass on Sundays and holy days. Keep these days holy and avoid unnecessary work.

2. Celebrate the Sacrament of Reconciliation at least once a year if there is serious sin.

3. Receive Holy Communion at least once a year during Easter time.

4. Fast and abstain on days of penance.

5. Give your time, gifts, and money to support the Church.

The Apostles' Creed

I believe in God, the Father almighty,
   creator of heaven and earth.
I believe in Jesus Christ, his only Son,
   our Lord.
   He was conceived by the power of the
      Holy Spirit
      and born of the Virgin Mary.
   He suffered under Pontius Pilate,
      was crucified, died, and was buried.
   He descended to the dead.
   On the third day, he rose again.
He ascended into heaven,
   and is seated at the right hand
      of the Father.
He will come again to judge the
   living and the dead.
I believe in the Holy Spirit,
   the holy catholic Church,
   the communion of saints,
   the forgiveness of sins,
   the resurrection of the body,
   and life everlasting. Amen.

The Nicene Creed

We believe in one God,
   the Father, the Almighty,
   maker of heaven and earth,
   of all that is, seen and unseen.
We believe in one Lord, Jesus Christ,
   the only Son of God,
   eternally begotten of the Father,
   God from God, Light from Light,
   true God from true God,
   begotten, not made, one in Being
      with the Father.
   Through him all things were made.
   For us men and for our salvation
      he came down from heaven:
   by the power of the Holy Spirit
      he was born of the Virgin Mary,
      and became man.
   For our sake he was crucified under
      Pontius Pilate;
   he suffered, died, and was buried.
   On the third day he rose again
      in fulfillment of the Scriptures;
he ascended into heaven
   and is seated at the right hand
      of the Father.
He will come again in glory to judge
   the living and the dead,
   and his kingdom will have no end.
We believe in the Holy Spirit, the Lord,
   the giver of life,
   who proceeds from the Father and
      the Son.
   With the Father and the Son he is
      worshiped and glorified.
   He has spoken through the Prophets.
We believe in one holy catholic and
   apostolic Church.
We acknowledge one baptism for the
   forgiveness of sins.
We look for the resurrection
   of the dead,
   and the life of the world to come.
Amen.

The Liturgical Year

In the liturgical year the Church celebrates Jesus' life, death, resurrection, and ascension through its seasons and holy days. The liturgical year begins with the First Sunday of Advent.

The readings for the entire Church year are contained in the Lectionary. Readings for Sundays and solemnities of the Lord are placed in a three-year rotation—Cycle A, Cycle B, and Cycle C.

The Season of Advent begins in late November or early December. During Advent we recall the first coming of the Son of God into human history, and we prepare for the coming of Christ—in our hearts, in history, and at the end of time. The liturgical color for Advent is violet.

On Christmas we celebrate the Incarnation, the Son of God becoming one of us. The color for Christmas is white, a symbol of celebration and life in Christ. (Any time white is used, gold may be used.)

Lent is the season of prayer and sacrifice that begins with Ash Wednesday and lasts about forty days. Lent has always been a time of repentance through prayer, fasting, and almsgiving. The liturgical color for Lent is purple, a symbol of penance.

Easter is the high point of the liturgical year because it celebrates Jesus' resurrection from the dead. The week beginning with Palm Sunday is called Holy Week. Lent ends on Holy Thursday evening, when the Easter Triduum begins. The Triduum, or "three holy days," includes the observance of Holy Thursday, Good Friday, and the Easter Vigil on Holy Saturday. The liturgical color for the Easter Season is white, a symbol of our joy in experiencing new life in Christ. The Easter Season lasts about seven weeks (fifty days).

At Pentecost, we celebrate the gift of the Holy Spirit sent to the followers of Jesus gathered in the upper room in Jerusalem. The liturgical color for Pentecost is red, a symbol of the tongues as of fire on Pentecost and of how Christ and some of his followers (such as the early Christian martyrs) sacrificed their lives for love of God.

The majority of the liturgical year is called Ordinary Time, a time when the Church community reflects on what it means to walk in the footsteps of Jesus. The liturgical color for Ordinary Time is green, a symbol of hope and growth.

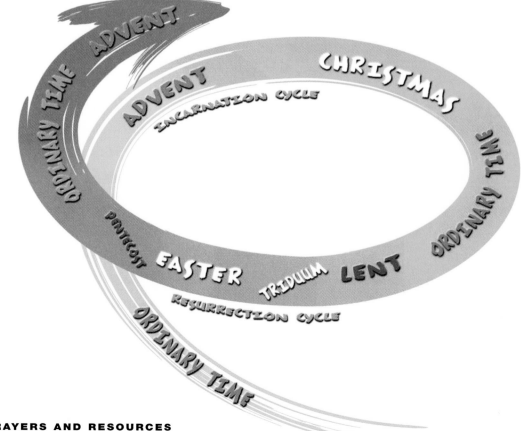

Glossary

A absolution — The forgiveness of sin we receive from God through the Church in the Sacrament of Reconciliation.

anoint — To use oil to mark someone as chosen for a special purpose.

C catechumen — An unbaptized person who has publicly stated his or her intention to become a member of the Church.

chrism — Sacred oil, made from olive oil scented with spices, used for anointing in the Sacraments of Baptism, Confirmation, and Holy Orders.

common priesthood — The whole community of believers who, through their participation in Jesus' gospel message, are members of the "holy priesthood."

communal prayer — Prayer that is prayed with others.

conscience — The gift from God that helps us know the difference between right and wrong and choose what is right. Conscience, free will, grace, and reason work together to help us in our decision making.

contrition — The deep sorrow and the resolve to do better that we feel when we have sinned; contrition moves us to turn our lives toward God.

conversion — The process of turning away from sin and evil and turning toward God.

covenant — A sacred and binding promise or agreement joining God and humans in relationship. Jesus' sacrifice established the new and everlasting covenant, open to all who do God's will.

D domestic Church — The Church as it exists within the family.

E Eucharist — The sacrament of Jesus' presence, which we celebrate by receiving his own Body and Blood under the form of bread and wine at Mass. From the Greek word meaning "gratitude," or "thanksgiving."

examination of conscience — A prayerful way of looking at our lives in light of the Ten Commandments, the Beatitudes, the life of Jesus, the teachings of the Church, and reason.

F funeral — The rites and ceremonies accompanying the burial of a deceased person.

G gifts of the Holy Spirit — The seven powerful gifts received in Baptism and strengthened in Confirmation that help us grow in our relationship with God and others. They are wisdom, understanding, counsel (right judgment), courage (fortitude), knowledge, reverence (piety), and wonder and awe (fear of the Lord).

godparent — The sponsor of a child at Baptism; one who promises to help the newly baptized person grow in faith.

grace — God's life in us through the Holy Spirit, freely given; our loving relationship with God; the free and undeserved help God gives us so that we may respond to the call to holiness.

L last rites — The celebration of the Sacraments of Reconciliation, Anointing of the Sick, and Eucharist by a person who is dying.

laying on of hands — A gesture used during the celebration of some sacraments to signify blessing, healing, invocation of the Holy Spirit, or conferral of office.

liturgical year — The annual cycle of Church seasons and feasts that comprise the Church year. The liturgical year, which does not correspond to the traditional calendar, celebrates Christ's life, death, resurrection, and ascension.

Liturgy of the Eucharist — The term for the entire celebration of the Mass as well as for the specific part of the Mass that includes the Preparation of the Gifts, the Eucharistic Prayer, and Communion.

Liturgy of the Word — The first great part of the Mass, lasting from the first reading to the General Intercessions, that celebrates God's word.

M ministerial priesthood — Ordained ministers of the Church who represent the presence of Christ to the faith community.

O original sin — The first humans' choice to disobey God and the condition that became a part of human nature whereby we are deprived of original holiness and justice; only Jesus and Mary, his mother, were free of original sin.

P Paschal mystery — The saving mystery of Jesus' passion, death, resurrection, and ascension.

Passover — An important Jewish holiday of thanksgiving; the day takes its name from the story of the Jewish Exodus from Egypt, during which the Lord spared, or "passed over," the Hebrew people.

penance — Prayers and actions undertaken to help us, in Christ, make up for the harm our sins have caused.

Pentecost — The descent of the Holy Spirit upon the apostles fifty days after Easter. The word *Pentecost* means "the fiftieth day."

personal prayer — Prayer that is prayed by an individual.

R rite — The established procedure for celebrating specific ceremonies in the Church.

S sacrament — A celebration in which Jesus joins with the assembled community in liturgical actions that are efficacious signs and sources of God's grace.

sacramentals — Sacred signs, which bear a resemblance to the sacraments, in that they make us aware of God's presence in our everyday lives. Blessings, holy water, candles, and the rosary are examples of sacramentals.

sacramental character — The spiritual and indelible mark we receive from the Holy Spirit during certain sacraments; it permanently changes our relationship to Christ and the Church.

Seal of the Holy Spirit — The spiritual and indelible character that comes from the Spirit through the anointing with chrism and accompanying words of the bishop.

sign — That which points to or explains something else.

sponsor — The person who presents the candidate for the anointing and promises to help him or her fulfill baptismal promises.

symbol — A sign that has effective emotional or spiritual meaning.

V viaticum — Holy Communion received as part of the last rites at the time of death. The word *viaticum* means "bread for the journey."

vocation — The call to live God's love in our everyday lives through the single life, marriage, the religious life, or the priesthood.

Index